Justice Delayed

Judicial Reform in Latin America

Edmundo Jarquín and Fernando Carrillo

Editors

Published by the Inter-American Development Bank
Distributed by the Johns Hopkins University Press

Washington, D.C.
1998

Cataloging-in-Publication data provided by the
Inter-American Development Bank
Felipe Herrera Library

Conferencia sobre Justicia y Desarrollo (2nd : 1995 : Montevideo, Uruguay)

Justice delayed : judicial reform in Latin America /
Edmundo Jarquín and Fernando Carrillo, editors.
p. cm.
Includes bibliographical references
ISBN: 1-886938-29-6
1. Law reform—Latin America—Congresses. 2. Law and economic development—Latin America—Congresses. 3. Justice, Administration of—Latin America—
Congresses. 4. International economic integration—Law and legislation—Congresses. I. Jarquín Calderon, Edmundo. II. Carrillo Flores, Fernando. III. Inter-American
Development Bank. IV. Title.
340.3 E37—dc20   97-77897

Contents

**PART III. INTERNATIONAL COOPERATION IN
JUDICIAL REFORM**

Introduction

Strengthening the rule of law in Latin America is crucial for achieving both democratic consolidation and economic efficiency. While democratic governments prevail in the region today, many difficulties confront the consolidation of democratic governance, not least in defining priorities and sequencing public policies. Inadequate laws and poorly functioning public institutions have exacted a high cost in terms of economic policy that the region's societies are no longer willing to pay. Economic development has increasingly clashed with the outmoded structure of state institutions, unreliable forms of government administration, and unsuitable public policies.

The role of government in the region has been changing—in terms of its dimensions, the nature of its interventions, and its relations with the private sector. Recognizing the relevance of state reform to their development agenda, Latin American countries continue to request that international organizations take action in these areas. The debate on state reform is now focused on standards of government performance and consolidating democratic governance. The Inter-American Development Bank has helped to define the terms of this debate, both in broad policies and through specific projects.

Toward the Effective Rule of Law

The Bank has emphasized the importance of democratic governance for implementing a solid policy of sustained and equitable development. Democratic governance presupposes socioeconomic cohesion, political freedoms, and guarantees of fundamental rights for all citizens, which determine whether democracy takes hold. Moreover, the processes of government are directly related to the sustainability of the economic model. Market activity alone does not produce fair competition or equity, which are fundamental for the market's legitimacy and for the democratic system. The institutions, laws, and regulations of a society should reflect the state's basic responsibilities in the pursuit of justice.

Governance, Rule of Law, and Development

The intrinsic relationship between development and governance is particularly relevant in the context of a market economy and democratic political systems. Private sector efforts to save, invest and innovate depend on a climate of stability and judicial security. Clearly defined rules of the game, with transparent scenarios that reduce transaction costs, are the basis of any effort to establish goals supportive of democracy and the market economy.

For Latin America's democracies, governance is linked to internal socio-economic integration, strong institutions, and citizen participation in the decision-making process. Governance is founded on several factors, including the following: a legal framework appropriate for development; the protection of fundamental citizen's rights, especially property rights; a suitable environment for the development of the private sector, with respect for freedom of contract; the efficient allocation of public resources; and responsible government with honesty and transparency at all levels of the state administration.

The Growing Role of Institutions

Public sector institutions in the region, while they are still fragile, are overcoming the problems that stem from macroeconomic disequilibria. This makes all the more evident the major shortcomings of government in performing public service functions and addressing citizens' expectations of services in the public interest.

Competitive and efficient markets, for example, can only develop on the basis of guarantees for property rights and the performance of contracts. There should be no opportunity for arbitrary government intervention that hinders market competition. At the same time, regulatory frameworks governing private activity are needed, to protect the public interest and establish general incentives for lawful behavior.

The construction of such frameworks begins with reform programs and initiatives in the legislatures, judiciaries, and the executive branch, as the Bank has emphasized. The judicial sector must implement procedures that diminish transaction costs and create adequate incentives for efficient operation. Above all, there is an urgent need for mechanisms that link effective rule of law with protection for the fundamental rights of citizens and public access to the justice system. To achieve these goals in the judicial sector, resources may need to be reallocated from less important areas of activity, or from tasks better performed by third parties. The state is neither the source of all solutions nor the cause of all problems. In the case of justice, however, its role is irreplaceable.

Judicial Reform

In 1993 the Inter-American Development Bank held a conference in Costa Rica, titled "Justice in Latin America and the Caribbean in the 1990s: Challenges and Opportunities." At that time the President of the Bank, Enrique Iglesias, set guidelines for future action, including analysis of the administration of justice in the Bank's programming and loans and technical cooperation projects in these new areas. The guidelines set forth have since been implemented, and the operation of these programs has made considerable strides. The issue of modernization and strengthening of the justice systems was incorporated in the Bank's Eighth General Increase in Resources, furthering fieldwork and analysis through the start-up of specific offices, such as the State and Civil Society Division. The conclusions of the Costa Rica meeting, published in book form in English and Spanish, were widely disseminated.

Since then, the administration of justice has been included in programming exercises carried out by the Bank with the countries. Workshops and activities were held to build consensus nationally and subregionally in countries such as Colombia, Honduras, Costa Rica, the Dominican Republic, Guatemala, and Peru, in direct dialogue not only with government entities, but also with civil society. At the regional level, evaluation workshops on judicial reform experiences have been sponsored in Washington, D.C., and Williamsburg, Virginia. Activities in 1997 included training judges in mechanisms for the protection of fundamental rights and evaluating reform strategies in Central America and South America.

International cooperation in these areas has also increased, as well as coordination among agencies such as the OAS, USAID, the UNDP, the European Union, the World Bank, and the Instituto de Cooperación Iberoamericana.

The Inter-American Bank is now sponsoring projects at different stages of preparation or implementation in Mexico, Guatemala, El Salvador, Costa Rica, Nicaragua, Honduras, Panama, the Dominican Republic, Colombia, Venezuela, Brazil, Ecuador, Peru, Argentine Chile, Uruguay, and Paraguay. These programs are adapted to the specific needs of different judicial systems, responding to needs on a country-by-country basis.

Lessons Learned

The key point in justice sector reform involves the actual structure of legal institutions and the rules that govern the exercise of the different branches of government. Consequently, the cornerstone of successful reform is the effective independence of the judiciary. That is a prerequisite for an impartial, efficient, and reliable judicial system. Without judicial independence, there is no rule of law, and without rule of law the conditions are not in place for the efficient operation of an open economy, so as to ensure conditions of legal and political security and foreseeability. This often presupposes working in the broad institutional context, such as constitutional and legislative reform, and the Bank has conceived of it in these terms in some projects. Judicial reform has political implications that must be tackled, and are of strategic importance in bringing the various social, political, and economic actors into the process.

In view of the foregoing, justice system reform cannot be limited to the judicial authorities. It must involve other institutions of the justice system beyond the judicial branch and lawmaking bodies as well, to adopt the legislation required. The authorities of the executive branch should also be committed, as they must provide the financial and administrative support necessary to move reform processes forward.

In terms of modernizing rules, access to justice, alternative dispute resolution, fighting judicial delays, new procedural forms, and information systems, operations should be "tailor-made," with strict adherence to specific national circumstances. The priorities of reform programs will vary, ranging from the complex problems of criminal justice to the need for decentralization and close cooperation with civil society.

Civil society is beginning to play a central part in judicial reform programs. Broad national consensus and political and business leadership is needed, as well as the support of political parties, civil society organizations and the mass media, to achieve favorable results. Judicial sector reform projects require much time and patience, and the results are gradual, entailing major cultural and institutional changes. Thus a major commitment from the countries themselves is a fundamental condition for judicial reform. Only with participation and "appropriation" by those involved will it be possible to advance. The Bank's many activities and efforts in various countries have corroborated this proposition.

Justice and Economy in Latin America

This book had its genesis in the Second Conference on Justice and Development, in Montevideo, Uruguay, in October 1995, whose participants included judicial and economic authorities, regional technical personnel, and university professors. The objective of this publication is to encourage debate on the fundamental role of the judicial system in economic development. A government subject to law, as well as a certain degree of legal security and an efficient justice system, are substantive requirements for consolidating democratic governance and for economic development.

In recent years, the countries of Latin America and the Caribbean have undertaken a process of structural change, including political, economic, and social change, in which judicial systems have taken growing initiative. The consolidation of democratic government and the operation of market forces require an independent, reliable, strong, efficient, equitable, and modern judicial system that not only ensures access to justice and protecting citizens rights, but also ensures a good climate for investment and growth. This legitimacy enables the judicial system to uphold the law and serve in its role as a check on the other branches of government.

The relationship between justice and economics has been the subject of recent research, as well as much speculation. There is a broad consensus among economists and jurists that the economic and social development of a country depends as much or more on its policies and institutions than on its natural resource base. One of the most important structures for institutionalizing policies is the legal structure. Legal systems, in turn, should reflect the social circumstances of each country, if they are to be effective and authoritative.

Given the circumstances and velocity of the changes under way in the region, it is imperative to implement a set of reforms that complement the conventional approaches to these processes of change, some of them already overtaken by the force of recent events. The new reforms must address even more subtle and complex issues such as the development of institutional capacity, modernization of the law, judicial system reform, the protection and defense of fundamental citizen rights, the struggle against corruption, the reform of the criminal justice systems, access to justice, and ways of controlling violence and guaranteeing citizen security.

Judicial reform includes redefining the role of the justice system itself. In this new environment it is necessary not only to frame the rules and codes, but also the political environment of the justice system and its administration and management, with managerial criteria, so as to be able to serve more appropriately the needs of a new political, economic, and social consensus.

The necessity for judicial reform coincides with processes of economic and political change on which the region has been embarked for over a decade. The legal and judicial framework must assimilate and face the realities of phenomena such as globalization and the internationalization of the economy.

The first part of this book concerns the relationship between justice and economics in the context of democratic consolidation. Néstor Humberto Martínez, in chapter one, highlights the importance of effective judicial systems and legal order that not only guarantee respect for individual and collective rights and liberties, but that also ensure the success of the economic reforms in the countries of the region. The lack of a solid and effective legal framework has a negative impact on investment, savings, and transaction costs, which makes judicial reform urgent. A reliable legal framework is necessary not only for domestic markets, but also for international markets. Another key point Martínez emphasizes is the relationship between credibility in the judicial system and economic efficiency.

Edgardo Buscaglia discusses the requirements of a modern and efficient judiciary adapted to needs imposed by the new economic reality. Buscaglia argues that the greatest impediments to reform of the system are to be found in the clientelistic practices, corruption, and existence of dispute resolution systems exercised by certain groups that benefit from an inefficient system. He notes the political impact of a dysfunctional legal-judicial framework: the lack of institutions and clear rules of the game open the way to political opportunism and personal enrichment, which has a damaging impact on the consolidation of democratic governance.

Robert Sherwood insists on the importance of analyzing how an ineffective judiciary affects economic development; in other words, how much less does a country grow because of the poor operation of its judicial system? Ricardo Hausmann undertakes a comparative analysis of judicial reform, drawing parallels among reforms to the justice system, the educational system, the economy (specifically, the reform that reduced inflation), and trade. Hausmann stresses the growing importance of adequate judicial entities for implementing economic reforms. The fundamental problem of judicial reform is the lack of an economic model to give it direction and provide an analysis of the causes of its ill-functioning, a clear strategy, and contents of the reform. Hausmann suggests that reform of the judicial system, unlike other areas (though similar to education) does not win support because its transformation takes time and its benefits are not immediate. In contrast to other programs, judicial reform does not have an alternative model for the organization and operation of the sector.

Rudolph Hommes, like Tomás Liendo, argues that judges, who are not part of the political process, should not impose responses on society just because they seem prudent or wise. The courts should move cautiously, and be "more willing to invent compromises than to declare firm and unambiguous principles." The position of these authors addresses the need to maintain a stable context for economic reforms.

In his paper, Santos Pastor points to the need for an assessment of the status of the system prior to any reform effort. To this end, he proposes an economic approach based on applied methods for obtaining information. This should allow a clearer evaluation of the situation, so as to focus on those areas that most require and allow for reform.

The second part of the book concerns the institutional environment of judicial systems. Hernando De Soto highlights the importance of guarantees for property rights in the context of the informal economy that has been characteristic of Latin American development. Luis Pásara analyzes judicial reform in the context of an increasingly active civil society, and examines the economic repercussions of judicial institutions that function efficiently, as Alberto Alesina reiterates with empirical evidence.

Jorge Correa Sutil emphasizes the growing importance of judicial systems, insofar as judges have the last say on many crucial political issues. He refers to challenges that confront the judicial system, among them fast-paced economic changes, globalization, state reform, and sociopolitical changes, ever more complex social systems and the active participation of various social actors with different demands. He explains the need to respond more flexibly and swiftly to needs that arise in view of such changes. Where the traditional response to demands, through strict application of the law, will not suffice, alternative dispute resolution mechanisms have the potential to maximize the interests at stake, and

yet hold parties accountable to one another, thereby encouraging their cooperation.

The last part of the book addresses the process of integration, economic
development, and the role of international organizations. Miguel Rodríguez Men-
doza emphasizes the new forms of integration of markets, goods, and services in
the region, and the role of the international organizations within this trend. The
experience of multilateral and bilateral cooperation agencies in judicial reform is
described by Ibrahim Shihata of the World Bank, Juan Antonio March Pujol of the
Instituto de Cooperación Iberoamericana, Paul Vaky of the U. S. Department of
Justice, Jorge Obando of the UNDP, and Fernando Carrillo of the IDB.

Conclusion

The contributors to this volume highlight the importance of the link between
strengthening the justice systems and promoting investment and growth in the
region. The dialogue on judicial reform must include economic authorities and
private sector leaders. Economic analysis should be applied to judicial reform
strategies, and the correlations between rule of law and efficiency in market economies must be demonstrated. An interdisciplinary approach to legal issues is needed to encompass the new realities of justice in Latin America.

The judicial reform strategies should take stock of the evaluations of a wide
array of lessons from reform efforts. Some of them are already clear. First, there
is need for comprehensive and long-term plans that include sectors of the justice
system with the most serious problems, such as those of criminal justice, prison
systems, and delinquent minors, or the population with least access to justice,
such as women, the poor, and indigenous peoples. Second, an improved institutional framework must be designed, recurring to legislative and constitutional
reform where necessary, for example, to assure the independence of the judiciary. Third, justice reform efforts need to be linked to civil society and to the other
branches of government and public agencies. Fourth, the infrastructure and information technology components, which have often contributed to disequilibria
in project objectives, must be adequately scaled. Fifth, there is a need for solid
consensus around the reform strategy that requires greater attention and resources
than projects in other sectors to ensure adequate implementation. And finally, the
economic relevance of these reform programs cannot be the sole justification for
the strategy, or its only application.

Many particular institutional experiences also need to be assimilated, especially with respect to the wide array of results in the region. Examples would be
the creation of judicial councils (*consejos de la judicatura* or *consejos de la
magistratura*) and the implementation of judicial career service systems, in principle immune to clientelism. A variety of prosecutorial offices have been set up in

the region to fight organized crime and battle corruption. It is no coincidence that 19 countries of Latin America and the Caribbean are moving from inquisitorial to accusatory or mixed systems, as the result of profound transformations under way in criminal justice. The judicial systems have also played a major role protecting citizens' fundamental rights. Institutions such as a national ombudsman for human rights are increasingly involved in rights-related disputes vis-à-vis the state. No single recipe applies to all the countries of the region, however. The various socioeconomic and political contexts will determine the content and strategy for each country's judicial reform.

Our assessment of strategy must be based on economic analysis, review of management practices, and results indicators, so as to ensure the new projects are on sure footing. What cannot be measured can hardly be well managed. While certain difficulties prevent rapid movement in that direction, justice system reform remains a top priority on the agenda of state reform and the strengthening of civil society, to create better conditions for the exercise of citizen rights.

We thank all those who made this publication possible, especially those who contributed their ideas. Special thanks to Sandra Bartels, for support in the first reading and adaptation of the texts; Ana María Schuett, of the State and Civil Society Division, for ensuring the material was pulled together in proper form; Gerardo Giannoni of the Publications Section for editing the Spanish text; and Eva Greene of Publications for editing the English text.

Edmundo Jarquín and Fernando Carrillo
Editors

PART I

JUSTICE AND
MARKET ECONOMIES

CHAPTER 1

Rule of Law and Economic Efficiency

Néstor Humberto Martínez

As this century closes, the structural pillars of a new international economic order are being defined. Its foundations provide support for the globalization of trade relations and technological exchange—what is sometimes referred to as the liberalization of market economies.

Latin America and the Caribbean are swiftly becoming part of this economic order, which offers new opportunities for development throughout the region. Yet there remain fundamental social and political challenges that, in our view, are essential complements to the neoliberal model of development. Liberal economic doctrine is not sufficient to ensure the kind of dynamic development that also yields benefits in terms of redistribution of wealth and greater social equity. The viability of the new model of economic growth is linked, we believe, to advances in the struggle against poverty and to the consolidation of democracy under the rule of law.

This chapter discusses the impact of judicial systems on economic growth, investment and savings, transaction costs, and the socioeconomic climate. Public perceptions of judicial systems are compared, and various reasons for public distrust of the judiciary. Finally, the chapter outlines an alternative vision for judicial reform and modernization.

Economic Growth

For the countries of Latin America and the Caribbean, sustaining the new economic model requires a legal order that is fair, efficient, easily accessible, and predictable. In the words of Michel Camdessus, ". . . without reducing their macroeconomic disciplines, governments should focus more on three essential areas: furthering reform of the state; making distributive justice an element of national economic policy; and promoting the cultural change implicit in and necessary for this transformation." We need effective judicial systems and legal order not only to guarantee respect for individual rights and freedoms, but also, and very significantly, to assure the success of reforms to our economies. Those who believe that macroeconomic adjustments and trade policy measures alone can redeem the performance of our economies and achieve the social benefits our peoples persistently demand, are wrong—very wrong.

Investment and Savings

The precarious nature of the legal framework, reflected in high crime rates and in the red tape required to defend one's rights, affects investment and long-term prospects for growth. This makes us more vulnerable to international competition and limits our capacity to carry out a process of modernization and industrial reconversion to remain competitive in international markets.

A recent study by the Colombian Ministry of Justice and Law concludes that investment is highly sensitive to "non-economic" factors. Moreover, such factors may have a greater impact on investment than certain economic variables have, such as the indicators of a trade opening or even the extent of financial deepening of a country. By adding specific non-economic variables to the investment function—such as the homicide rate, which is very high in Colombia—one obtains significant statistical outcomes. For every increase of 10 homicides per 100,000 population, investment falls 4 percent (Rubio 1995).

Under imperfect legal systems, savings are also more volatile. Difficulties in judicial systems are reflected in lesser degrees of financial deepening. Given the legal risks, savers seek to protect themselves by limiting the amounts of their deposits, or at least limiting their terms. In the marketplace, various kinds of insurance can protect savings from risk, but there is no protection against court delays or wrongful judgments.

Transaction Costs

One of the legal system's most harmful problems is inefficiency—the added transaction costs associated with not knowing the rules to follow or the case law that applies. Estimating the time required to obtain recognition of a right is difficult, as well as the degree to which judicial decisions are foreseeable. Entrepreneurs must include these transaction costs in their prices for both domestic and international markets, which damages their competitive status in those markets.

To see this phenomenon in proper context, a few cases will illustrate the problem:

- Where judicial systems introduce new rules to compensate for administrative deficiencies, the rules that regulate business activity are in constant flux. In addition to other problems this causes, it requires businessmen to invest excessive sums of human resources and capital in order to adapt to new regulations and statutes. In Colombia, changing statutes and regulations account for up to 45 percent of the variations in GDP growth between 1954 and 1988 (Rubio 1995). For an international sample of 28 countries, a World Bank study reports that the degree of credibility and stability in the rules and procedures of the various legal systems can explain 23 percent of the variation in per capita growth (Weder 1994). This sort of legal uncertainty means that the most talented entrepreneurs in society must dedicate themselves to studying and evading the laws, rather than producing (Montenegro 1994).

- Collecting bank obligations through executory proceedings is a slow and expensive process. While assets are tied up in litigation, financial institutions are forced to cover losses that might occur in their balance sheets by higher interest rates, to distribute these losses among their borrowers. In fact, based on the balance sheets of the Colombian banking system as of December 31, 1994, one may conclude that due to inefficiencies in the justice apparatus, the debtors of the national banking system are assuming a cost greater than the usual price of credit, equivalent to one-half point of the margin for financial intermediation.

- The lack of prompt and effective guarantees for property rights drives up the costs required for property owners to enjoy and use their assets. A good example is rental leases, which now cost so much that they are inaccessible to certain sectors of the population. This is because lessors must insure themselves against the cost of eviction proceedings, in the event they must repossess their property.

- Impunity from criminal prosecution also takes a very high toll on a country's productivity. Each actor, in his stage of production or marketing, covers himself from the risks of criminal activity, and all the more so when the prospects for punishment are uncertain. To illustrate, Colombians pay annual automobile insurance premiums that total 0.7 percent of the GDP.

- Another set of transaction costs, wherever judicial systems are weak, is the business expenditures entailed by corruption. The bribes or extortion known as *coima*, *serrucho*, *el diez por ciento*, and *mordida* operate, in effect, as extralegal taxes on productive activity.

Socioeconomic Environment

If a given legal order cannot effectively re-establish equity in civil disputes between stronger and weaker parties (as, for example, entrepreneurs and workers), this worsens the relations between capital and labor. Wherever criminal courts are ineffective, crime rates rise, and this has a markedly negative effect on growth, factor productivity, and capital formation. Using regression models, Rubio (1994) estimates that the increase in crime from 20 homicides per 100,000 population in 1970 to more than 80 per 100,000 in the 1990s is costing Colombia some 2 percent annually in GDP growth.

Perceptions of Justice

At present, public trust in the justice system in our region is very low. Less than 30 percent of our people (with the exception of Costa Rica, the Dominican Republic, and Uruguay) express satisfaction with how the justice system works. By contrast, Table 1.1 indicates that in countries with a greater real per capita GDP, more than 50 percent of the citizens have confidence in the justice system. There is a positive correlation, then, between trust in the justice system and social well-being. Clearly, a nation's socioeconomic development is linked to the institutional arrangements, order, and legality of government under the rule of law. If judicial systems can respond to the public demand for speedy and effective justice, economies in transition will be able to benefit far more from macroeconomic reforms.

The view of those who are served by the justice system is important, for more than merely academic reasons. The public behaves according to a certain economic rationale. When the administration of justice is viewed critically, this affects the efficiency of the entire economy, for the reasons already mentioned. But why do citizens have this collective vision of our justice systems? Some possible answers are as follows:

Lack of Knowledge and Distrust of Laws

If the Colombian case is any indication, lack of knowledge and distrust of the laws may be rooted in legislative "inflation"—which, like monetary inflation, corrodes the value of the legal rules—and the greater discretion in their issuance. A study of the "demography of laws" in Colombia, undertaken at the initiative of the Ministry of Justice and Law, concludes that:

- From 1950 to 1988, the total number of laws to which enterprises were subject grew 3.5 percent annually. From 1989 to 1994, this rate of growth increased to 9 percent annually. In other words, the number of laws used to double every 20 years, but now is doubling every eight years.
- For laws pertaining to businesses, the percent issued by regulatory discretion has increased continuously, to approximately 75 percent in 1994. Of every four articles that regulate business, three are non-legislative in origin.
- The average life span of the laws dropped, between 1989 and 1994, from 20 to 14 years.

Such an excess of regulations and interventionism leads to ignorance of the law. The resulting legal anomie creates confusion and uncertainty; one cannot know if today's law will still be in effect tomorrow. This becomes a disincentive to long-term investment decisions, which require stable rules of the game.

Table 1.1 Public Trust and Per Capita GDP, 1991

(Percent of population)

Country	Degree of trust	Real per capita GDP ($US)
Japan	68	19,390
Germany	67	19,770
United Kingdom	66	16,340
France	55	18,430
Uruguay	53	6,670
United States	51	22,130
Italy	43	17,040
Spain	41	12,670
Costa Rica	39	5,100
Dominican Republic	33	3,080
Chile	27	7,060
Colombia	26	5,460
El Salvador	25	2,110
Mexico	22	7,170
Venezuela	22	8,120
Bolivia	21	2,170
Peru	21	3,110
Ecuador	16	4,140
Guatemala	15	3,180

Source: Lemoine, C. 1994. "Public Confidence in Institutions." *Human Development Report 1994*, UNDP.

Access to Justice Is Limited

The lack of access to justice, due to cultural, economic, geographic, and social barriers, has created a new type of marginalization and social exclusion. When such barriers are reflected in legal outcomes, this undermines the social legitimacy of the judicial and legal system.

Crime Is Not Effectively Deterred

Crime is a growing international problem, and the capacity of governments to deter crime is not increasing When citizens see crime on the rise, they understand that it threatens their own security, and this strongly affects their perceptions of the justice system. In our region, there are long delays before obtaining judgments against those accused of crimes. This is indicated by comparing the number of persons imprisoned and awaiting trial, with the number of those charged or convicted (Table 1.2). On average about 80 percent of the prison population has been processed.

Justice Is Slow

If the public believes that judicial proceedings are burdensome and slow, statistics bear them out. With few exceptions, a regular civil trial, in both trial and appellate phases, takes more than two years (Table 1.3). In other words, the cost of resolving a dispute is very high.

Demand Outstrips Supply

Despite efforts to accommodate the institutional capacity of the state to offer better judicial services, the reforms carried out have been insufficient. The demand for court services is on the rise. Among the reasons for this are greater public awareness, mounting social conflict, increased contacts between urban and rural life, a growing number of lawyers, and the development of actions to protect collective rights. In the face of a practically inelastic supply, the annual levels of retention of cases increases, as Table 1.4 indicates. Thus the backlog of cases awaiting trial, now growing exponentially, seriously affects the performance of the judiciary.

Economic Imperatives of Judicial Reform

In order to assure the success and sustainability of economic reform, judicial reform is imperative. This section outlines an alternative, complementary vision for judicial reform. It is both alternative and complementary, because the traditional processes of modernizing the justice system have run their course and are increasingly incompatible with the policies for handling the public treasury. In some cases it will be legitimate to seek more resources for the proper functioning of the justice system. Table 1.5 indicates that some countries invest much less in their justice systems than others. In Europe, for example, 4 to 5 percent of the regular budget is spent on the justice sector; in the United States, the criminal justice system alone receives 3 percent of the federal budget. Nevertheless, the public sector in the region is undergoing times of austerity, and creativity is being put to a test.

Nor will it be possible to stem the demands from the sector by increasing

Table 1.2 Efficiency of the Criminal Justice System
(Percentage of the inmate population accused or convicted)

Country	Percent	Years
Argentina	82.00	1992
Chile	49.32	1993
Colombia	56.00	1995
El Salvador	>80.00	1993
Panama	>90.00	1993
Paraguay	92.12	1994
Uruguay	80.00	1993
Venezuela	66.10	1994

Source: For Argentina, Paraguay, and Uruguay, IDB Legal Department, July 1994. Juan Enrique Vargas Viancos, "Diagnóstico del sistema judicial chileno," 1995. Ministry of Justice and Law of Colombia, "Justicia para la gente," 1995. For El Salvador and Panama, José María Rico and Luis Salas, *La administración de la justicia en América Latina. Una introducción al sistema penal*, 1993. For Venezuela, *Situación y políticas judiciales en América Latina*, Law School of the Diego Portales University, Bogotá, Colombia, 1993.

Table 1.3 Duration of Civil Proceedings
(Average regular civil proceedings, trial and appellate stages)

Country	Average
Argentina	> 2 years (45% cases)
Chile	2 years 9 months
Colombia	2 years 9 months
Costa Rica	10 months 1 week
Paraguay	> 2 years
Peru	4 years 6 months
Uruguay [a]	8 months

[a] Uruguay is an exception, due to the success of its procedural reforms in 1989.
Source: For Argentina, Costa Rica, Paraguay, Peru, and Uruguay, IDB Legal Department, July 1994. Juan Enrique Vargas Viancos, "Diagnóstico del sistema judicial chileno," 1995. Ministry of Justice and Law of Colombia, "Justicia para la gente," 1995.

Table 1.4 Backlog of Cases

Country	Year	Percentage of cases postponed
Argentina	1991	94.0
Bolivia	1993	50.0
Chile	1989	5.7
Colombia	1994	37.0
Ecuador	1990	42.0
Peru	1993	59.0

Source: For Argentina, Bolivia, Ecuador, and Peru, IDB Legal Department, July 1994. Juan Enrique Vargas Viancos, "Diagnóstico del sistema judicial chileno," 1995. In Chile the figure represents the average of *juzgados de partido* (trial courts) (44 percent) and *juzgados de instrucción* (preliminary investigative courts) (55 percent) for civil matters. "Actividad judicial en Colombia, 1993-1994," Consejo Superior de la Judicatura, 1995.

the number of judges and other judicial staff for fiscal reasons, among others. In addition, in many cases the relevance of doing so is not very clear, all the more so when one surpasses the international average, or the indicator for the number of judges per 100,000 population in countries such as Spain and the United States, as illustrated in Table 1.6. Expanding the number of judges and judicial staff has been a common remedy in our systems, with limited resources in most cases. Given this state of affairs, we believe that the judicial reform should be broadened to encompass concepts such as the following:

Modernizing Judicial Management

The judicial system is a public service that should be administered using modern managerial techniques, yet it is significantly behind in this respect. Investment in the sector can play a catalytic role by modernizing the judicial branch's management system, as follows:

• Adequate sectoral planning that involves all interested actors and authorities, to allocate existing resources more efficiently in light of clearly defined priorities and purposes.
• A method of government within the judiciary that is expeditious, efficient, logical, and accountable. In other words, it should be answerable to different parts of the state and to society as a whole.
• Bolstering the professionalism of the judicial administration.

Table 1.5 Resources Allocated to Justice Systems, 1993-1994

Country	Percent of budget allocated to justice
Costa Rica	5.50
Colombia	4.62
El Salvador	4.50
Bolivia	3.00
Ecuador	2.50
Uruguay	1.52
Paraguay	1.50
Argentina	1.47
Honduras	1.00
Chile	0.75
Panama	0.50

Sources: IDB Legal Department, 1994, and calculations by the Ministry of Justice and Law, Colombia.

Table 1.6 Number of Judges per 100,000 Population, 1993

Country	Judges per 100,000
Colombia[1]	17.1
Uruguay	15.5
Argentina	11.0
Costa Rica	11.0
El Salvador	9.0
Bolivia	8.0
Nicaragua	7.8
Ecuador	4.7
Chile	3.8
Guatemala	3.0
Spain	3.0
United States	2.0
Netherlands	2.0

[1] Includes judges and prosecutors.
Source: UN, IDB, and calculations by Colombian Ministry of Justice and Law.

Table 1.7 Alternative Dispute Resolution Mechanisms, 1994

Country	Extrajudicial mechanisms
Argentina	Mediation, conciliation, and arbitration (private systems) Out-of-court settlement
Bolivia	Arbitration
Chile	Arbitration
Colombia	Direct settlements (not provided for by law) Conciliation, mediation, and arbitration Friendly settlement Neutral case evaluation
Costa Rica	Arbitration
Ecuador	Arbitration and conciliation (private mechanisms) Out-of-court settlement
Paraguay	Arbitration
Peru	Arbitration
Uruguay	Arbitration

Source: IDB Legal Department, for all countries except Chile (Juan Enrique Vargas Viancos, "Diagnóstico del sistema judicial chileno," 1995) and Colombia (Ministry of Justice and Law of Colombia, "Justicia para la gente," 1995).

• Comprehensive data collection systems to provide the information required by the planning and management agencies.

Strengthening Alternative Systems

The formal supply of justice needs to be increased through alternative dispute resolution systems: out-of-court settlement, mediation, conciliation, arbitration, friendly settlement, justices of the peace, or neighborhood judges. Table 1.7 shows that there is much room for work on these types of alternatives, which play a significant role in the developed countries.

Training and Reappraisal of Human Resources

Efforts to modernize the judicial sector must extend to its human resources—those who work within or cooperate with judicial systems. Training citizens must also be included, as citizens need to know their rights and should be able to make proper and rational use of the service. Legal education should place more emphasis on the culture of compromise and conciliatory settlement of disputes. Judges and other judicial staff should be given opportunities for continuing education in the context of a stable, career-based system that provides incentives for their ongoing professional training.

We must reappraise the social sectors and state institutions. Sustainable and integrated development can only be achieved through the balanced and symmetric action of all the sectors. We must make certain that the costs of judicial reform are not merely additional expenses, but represent an investment that complements the structural economic reforms that can no longer be deferred.

References

Montenegro, A. 1994. Justicia y desarrollo económico. Mimeo, Departamento Nacional de Planeación, Colombia.

Rubio, M. 1995. Crimen y crecimiento en Colombia. *Coyuntura económica* 25:1.

———. 1994. Crimen y justicia en Colombia—Un enfoque económico. *Revista de derecho privado* 8:15.

Weder, B. 1994. Legal Systems and Economic Performance: The Empirical Evidence. World Bank Conference on Judicial Reform in Latin America and the Caribbean, June 1994.

CHAPTER 2

Obstacles to Judicial Reform in Latin America

Edgardo Buscaglia

Political progress and economic liberalization in Latin America and the Caribbean have sparked renewed interest in reform of the public sector. One area that needs serious reform is the judicial system, which is a key factor in establishing the rule of law. Democratization, growing urbanization, and the adoption of market reforms have all led to additional demands for court services throughout the region. As social interactions grow more complex, better means of resolving conflicts are required. In addition, most economic transactions are shifting to the market and outside the public sector, so that rights and obligations need to be more clearly defined.

What Is Meant by Judicial Reform

The rule of law is necessary to ensure the political stability of liberal democracy.[1] Only by establishing an enforceable, compulsory, and foreseeable rule of law will the countries of Latin America become strong and competitive democracies. An independent judiciary is essential for the separation of powers. This is particularly relevant for the presidential forms of government prevalent in Latin America. Most of the region's judiciaries are weak, overly politicized, and dependent on the executive power, and thus do not provide effective oversight and control of other branches of government. If there is to be a lasting consolidation of liberal democracy, the notion of democratic rights (both civil and political rights) should come to be assumed and take root socially. This requires the existence of an impartial and predictable court system capable of providing equitable protection of rights and effective administration of justice. The quality of a liberal democracy is deeply affected by the relations between state and society and, in a broader sense, by the rule of law.

---

[1] Guillermo O'Donnell (1993) explains the importance of the rule of law to strengthen democratic institutions in Latin America.

Moreover, the judicial system is key to economic development. Through the courts, both the public and private sectors interpret the laws and regulations applying to market transactions. The judiciary's main role in the economic system is to resolve conflicts within the procedural and substantive structure that facilitates exchanges of rights in physical and intangible values. In most Latin American countries, however, the courts suffer mounting delays, backlogs, and corruption, which leads the private sector and the general public to distrust the system.[2] In addition, lack of access to a fair and efficient judicial system creates additional uncertainties and hinders the consummation of beneficial transactions, all of which harms private investment. In the absence of an impartial and efficient judiciary, mutually beneficial transactions will take place only where there is a well-sustained reputation or where the parties have already engaged in repeated transactions. This requirement excludes many potential transactions, such as those involving new partners or start-up businesses.

The economic stabilization and liberalization policies adopted throughout Latin America in the 1980s require a predictable legal framework and a judiciary capable of applying those laws effectively and fairly. Sustained long-term growth and development require more than stabilization policies. The state must be able to provide a predictable and reliable legal context. Economic liberalization and privatization policies alone will not provide the appropriate conditions for economic development. There must also be sufficient political and legal stability— whose best guarantee is the effective rule of law.

The poor social and economic conditions in much of Latin America, extreme socioeconomic inequality, and social and cultural divisions exacerbate the heterogeneity of the region's civil societies (Argentina, Chile, and Uruguay being the most homogeneous). Most Latin American populations are indeed fragmented, with stark differences in awareness of the formal and institutional procedures of democratic citizenship. Assimilating the principles of democratic rights and the rule of law is much more difficult for a resident of the rural areas of Bolivia or Guatemala than for an urban middle-class professional from Buenos Aires or São Paulo.

The public is increasingly aware that democratic rights should be protected and respected. Nevertheless, surveys throughout the region indicate that judicial institutions have low prestige and are viewed as incompetent.[3] The growing awareness of individual rights is due partly to activism for democracy, the work of non-

---

[2] The *World Competitiveness Report* (1994) compares public trust in the judicial systems of 35 developed and developing countries. All Latin American countries except Chile rank in the lowest 15 percent for public trust.

[3] Public opinion polls throughout the region portray judges as corrupt and the judicial decision-making process as inconsistent. See Buscaglia and Dakolias (1995).

governmental organizations, and international criticism of human rights abuses. Institutions such as the National Commission on Human Rights in Mexico and Poder Ciudadano in Argentina play a significant role in ensuring these rights are protected.

The international financial community is increasingly concerned with the issues of judicial reform and strengthening the legal institutions in the new democratic states. The most exhaustive judicial reforms in the region have occurred in Argentina, Chile, Colombia, Costa Rica, Ecuador, and Venezuela. Exhaustive judicial reform must include all hierarchies of the judicial system, and should be aimed at the following areas: (i) improvements in the administration of justice; (ii) strengthening the independence of the judiciary; (iii) developing alternative dispute resolution mechanisms (i.e. mediation, arbitration, conciliation boards, etc.); (iv) improving the legal education of judges, lawyers, and the general public; and (v) creating new channels so that vast sectors of the population, now excluded, can have access to justice.

Wherever exhaustive reforms have been proposed, the business sectors associated with foreign investment are supporting it.[4] There is growing awareness that strong legal institutions are needed as a basis for economic planning. Consistent and predictable application of legal rules would be a powerful incentive for potential foreign investors. Effective legal and constitutional protection of property rights would increase business confidence. Nonetheless, support is not strong from local businesses, which still oppose certain reforms that would eliminate some of their present advantages, such as the discretionary practices of a developing capitalist state, where judicial scrutiny is not effective.

The way these different pressures operate, and the weight of the interests at stake, will influence the nature and the pace of the legal reforms, and the types of court services most susceptible to improvement. Thus, major improvements can be expected in the judicial services provided in the commercial courts, which are used by firms associated with foreign investors. But unless access to justice is available for the very large marginalized sectors of society—where local vested interests, such as clientelist political fiefs, prevail—efforts to strengthen the liberal democracies of the region will be frustrated.

Despite the obvious convenience of a justice system that works and the rule of law, Latin American countries face formidable obstacles to reforming their judicial systems. Buscaglia and Dakolias (1995) observe that the gaps in the formal legal codes and in the constitutional norms are not the root of the problem of

---

[4] In a World Bank survey of 68 companies operating in the region, the most serious barriers to private sector development in Latin America were listed as follows: political instability, inflation, regulatory barriers, ineffective judicial systems, lack of qualified labor, lack of infrastructure, high tax rates, access to loans, and lack of services. See Buscaglia and Dakolias (1995).

the dysfunctional administration of justice. Where exhaustive judicial reforms have been proposed, they are often opposed by entrenched vested interests, which benefit precisely from the absence of the rule of law. For democratic consolidation (politically and socially) as well as for long-term economic stability and growth, a minimally impartial and independent judiciary is needed, and a justice system that operates at all levels. Thus this chapter seeks to identify the main obstacles to implementing judicial reform throughout the region.

Some problems related to the delivery of services by the courts may be the direct result of legislation (procedural or substantive laws) or the lack of legislation. Inadequate infrastructure and insufficient resources (i.e., capital, personnel, goods and services) can also impair the functioning of the judicial system. A third category of problems normally arises from already established practices based on clientelism, private interests, or blatant corruption. These interrelated factors tend to undermine any systematic effort to improve the quality of the legal services provided to the general population. The judicial history of many countries of Latin America highlights precisely the failures of the reforms that did not study problems created by the personal interests that frustrate judicial reforms. Implementation of judicial reforms ultimately depends on those involved in providing legal services. This paper will address some of the problems that result from long-entrenched interests in the justice system that benefit from the relative absence of an independent and impartial judiciary.

Characteristics of Latin America's Judicial Systems

The judicial sector in Latin America would seem ill-prepared to foster the development of the private sector in a market economy. Results of questionnaire surveys of Latin American firms indicate that the judicial system is considered one of the ten most significant limitations on the development of the private sector.[5] The basic elements of an effective judicial system are absent, namely: (i) consistent and relatively predictable decisions; (ii) access to courts for the population, irrespective of income; (iii) reasonable time for the disposition of cases; and (iv) adequate remedies.

Mounting delays, case backlogs, and the uncertainty of results have diminished the quality of justice throughout the region. Among the obstacles facing the judiciary are dysfunctional administration of justice, lack of transparency, and a perception of corruption. Delays and corruption in the judicial systems of Latin America have reached unprecedented proportions.[6] In 1993, for example, the av-

---

[5] The results indicate that in samples of 60 to 100 companies per country, most of the companies consider that the role played by the judiciary is "deficient."
[6] See CIA (1994).

erage times for disposition of cases in the civil courts in Argentina, Ecuador, and Venezuela were 6.5 years, 7.9 years, and 8.4 years, respectively—an increase of 85 percent since 1981. The standard deviations of the times for the disposition of cases for Argentina, Ecuador, and Venezuela are 1.1 years, 0.9 years, and 1.9 years, respectively. These differentials increased at an alarming rate in the last decade. There is lack of uniformity in the quality of the services and unequal distribution of caseloads among different courts.

According to Table 2.1, these delays worsened from 1983 to 1993 compared with the previous ten years, which explains public dissatisfaction with the judicial systems throughout the region. This table also explains why a recent survey of the region's judicial systems indicates that most citizens "are not inclined" to bring disputes before the courts, because they consider the system slow, unsafe, and expensive or "low-quality." This lack of confidence is more pronounced among small economic units and low-income families.[7]

Improving the capacity of the courts to handle caseloads is a major challenge for judicial reform efforts. In most of Latin America the courts seem inadequate to perform their most basic function, for interpreting and applying the law. The inability to meet this demand is expressed in an increasing backlog of cases, and in the delays that can be observed throughout the region. While these delays may be due in part to procedural defects, other may include the lack of legal training, the lack of an active style of case management, and excessive administrative burdens on judges. For example, in Argentina approximately 70 percent of judges' time is taken up in tasks not related to their judgeship (Buscaglia and Dakolias 1995). These same administrative tasks take up 65 and 69 percent of available judicial time in Brazil and Peru, respectively. Judges are not the only court personnel who suffer the imposition of excessive administrative requirements. According to recent surveys of the courts in Ecuador, Venezuela, Peru, and Argentina, from 20 to 40 percent of court staff interviewed appear to be pleased to receive administrative assignments, such as signing checks or ordering office supplies. The explanation may lie in the fact that administrative tasks give the judges a false sense of autonomy and planning capability.[8]

Judges with limited training working in an overburdened judicial system are also susceptible to corrupting influences and create an environment in which the rule of law cannot be guaranteed. The widespread use of ex parte communications in Latin American courts contributes to this perception. When communication with only one of the parties is permitted and even encouraged, the parties in conflict can approach the judges, and the judges may request to see the parties

---

[7] See Buscaglia and Ulen (1995).
[8] See Jesse Cassaus (1994).

Table 2.1 Case Delay and Backlog, Federal Commercial and Civil Jurisdictions

(Percent change)

Country	Average delay		Backlog	
	1973-82	1983-93	1973-82	1983-93
Argentina	16.7	47.8	9.2	47.9
Brazil	n.d.	39.1	2.2	19.7
Chile	8.4	11.1	12.1	29.4
Colombia	3.4	27.8	9.1	28.1
Mexico	n.d.	n.d.	7.2	34.1
Venezuela	3.1	48.3	11.8	51.3

Sources: Statistics Office of the Supreme Court of Justice of Argentina, 1994 Annual Report; Office of Judicial Statistics of Chile, 1993 Annual Report; Office of Court Statistics of the Ministry of Justice of Brazil, 1994 Annual Report; Office of Court Statistics of the Ministries of Justice of Colombia and Venezuela, 1990-1994.

or their attorneys separately. There are accusations of cases that have been decided in such meetings.

All the above problems also add costs and risks to business transactions, and therefore reduce the potential size of key markets. At the same time, access to justice is blocked for all those unable to pay the cost of delays or simply the price imposed by corruption (for example, bribes).[9]

Obstacles to Reform

Only by identifying the factors that encourage or hinder judicial reform can one propose policies to modernize the judiciary. Those factors include not only the social costs and benefits of reforms, but also changes in individual rents received by court personnel and other government employees. This part examines two key elements for implementing judicial reform: identifying the causes of the insti-

---

[9] Many national constitutions of the region (e.g., Ecuador), provide for a free legal system, with no charges or fees whatsoever. Even though the courts are theoretically accessible to all, abolishing the fees contributes to the problem of low salaries, inefficacy, and poor quality. The lack of formal legal fees creates incentives for court employees to charge unauthorized fees. A litigant may be requested to pay a fee to move his case along—a monetary transaction that personally benefits a judge or judicial employee. This contributes to the system's corruption, and in practice denies access to the courts.

tutional inertia that is an obstacle to much-needed reforms of the courts; and analyzing why reforms occur in some places but not in others, by reference to the costs and benefits of implementing judicial reforms, as members of the courts perceive them.

In order to win public confidence, reform efforts should address the legal, economic, and political causes of an ineffective and unjust judiciary, not just the symptoms. The basic elements of judicial reform should thus include the following: improvements in court administration and day-to-day case management; redefining and/or expanding legal education programs and programs for preparing students, lawyers, and judges; greater facilities for ensuring public access to justice through legal aid programs and legal education, geared to fostering public awareness as to rights and obligations once one avails oneself of the courts; the availability of alternative dispute resolution mechanisms, such as arbitration, mediation, and conciliation; judicial independence (i.e. budgetary autonomy, transparency in the appointments process, and job stability), which goes hand-in-hand with a transparent disciplinary system for judicial personnel; and the adoption of procedural reforms where necessary. Each component is an integral part of the overall judicial reform. Not all components can be addressed at the same time, but a program of action should take account of the costs and benefits of reform, as perceived by the members of the judiciary.

Political Instability

The obstacles to judicial reform are deeply rooted in the political, social, and economic environment in which the legal systems developed. Political instability, for example, has been a recurring problem in the past. The collapse of regimes, authoritarianism, and repeated violations of basic principles of liberal democracy, have contributed to the institutional instability of the judiciary and the justice system in Latin America.

In the past, military regimes impaired the judicial branch in several ways: by undermining its independence; by destabilizing the terms of appointments and tenure of judges; and by perverting the notion of the rule of law through overtly illegal activities. Abuse of human rights is the worst case of the illegal activities of military governments. Failure to abide by the law and lack of transparency in economic management are also problematic under a military regime, in many cases creating mounting friction within the upper levels of the judiciary.

Long-term political instability, as in Bolivia, has prevented the judicial branch from establishing institutional authority in its own right. Only recently, with the advent of democratization, have the region's supreme courts begun to exercise political weight. There are exceptions, such as Chile, where democratic stability was the norm for much of the 20th century before Pinochet's dictatorship. Chile's judiciary had enjoyed considerable prestige, despite its enormous isolation from the rest of society due to lack of transparency in appointments and in the rules of the game.[10] Therefore, reestablishing a sense of legality is different in Chile as compared to countries where the judiciary did not enjoy that prior legacy of institutional independence and strength. In Colombia as well, formal institutions have not been subject to continuous convulsions, so that country's judiciary enjoys a reputation for relative independence.[11] Mexican courts, however, despite the relative political stability over the last 50 years, cannot by any stretch of the imagination be considered politically independent; rather, the judiciary has traditionally been subordinated to the executive.

While many countries of the region have done relatively well in terms of selective democratic criteria (e.g., free and competitive elections), the question of judicial and legal reform continues to be problematic. Clearly, judicial reform occupies a high place in the region's political agenda. More recently some courts have achieved a higher political profile, in the midst of corruption scandals involving persons in high-level public positions. As democratic rules begin to apply, their impact will extend beyond short-term electoral coalitions and agreements on the rules of the regime, and should eventually include judicial scrutiny over public offices.

The political impact of a dysfunctional legal-judicial framework is extremely complex. The lack of solid legal institutions leaves much room for political opportunism and personal enrichment, not subject to public or judicial scrutiny, precisely because of the lack of transparency in applying the law, and the absence of checks and balances. The problem of impunity and corruption among the political elites is problematic for democratic consolidation in the long run, and poses major questions regarding regime credibility and legitimacy. This is particularly true in times of scarce resources, which are typical of the economic austerity packages that have accompanied the economic liberalization policies. The effect has been a reduction in the redistributive capacity or the opportunities for self-enrichment through clientelist relationships with and within the state. As a result of this reduction in potential rents during times of austerity, the power of vested interests opposed to judicial reforms has diminished.

The deeply-rooted political habit of flouting the law is at the same time a symptom of and a problem for judicial system reform. Political discourse includes great enthusiasm for reforming the justice system. Nonetheless, not even well-intentioned legislation will necessarily be effectively implemented. First is the difficulty of overcoming the practice of impunity, even when it does not amount

---

[10] See Jorge Correa Sutil (1992).
[11] See Salas and Rico (1993) and Jesse Cassaus (1994).

to total corruption. Second, the judicial reform is a promising political card until it faces specific political barriers (i.e., when the reform represents a threat to those who hold power). And finally, even if there is a firm government commitment to the reform, the problem of its implementation will persist so long as irregular practices and impunity are endemic throughout the political system.

Corruption

The problem of corruption reflects, first, the inability of the public sector to establish an authoritative legal order. In addition, corruption flourishes where clientelist relations prevail in the state institutions, in the various interest groups, and among private persons. In this context, corruption is transmitted through the organizational structures and reinforced by the external effects of their networks. If the awarding of public posts is not merit-based—rather, one finds a politicized bureaucracy that is poorly paid and ill-trained—corruption will inevitably result, and the external relations of the network will foster such corruption by increasing their proportional share. This is a consequence of the lack of mechanisms to ensure accountability and judicial scrutiny. It presents a powerful obstacle to implementing legal reforms capable of threatening a network of mutually beneficial relations.

In the justice system corruption takes the form of bribery, political pressure, and personal influence at different levels. It is closely associated with infrastructure problems: low salaries, instability in the post, lack of a professional merit-based evaluation, and also long-established practices according to which the law does not apply equally to everyone. In addition, and related to the problem of public order, is the extent of drug trafficking and the way in which it has infiltrated the state institutions at various levels. The authoritarian capacity of the state to confront infiltration by the mafia in public posts is seriously undermined by the vast capital they control. If combined with a tradition of impunity for public officeholders, this presents a formidable obstacle to effective legal reform.

Though it is debatable, recent experiences show that with democratization, impunity does not always go unpunished (as in the case of the impeachment of Collor de Mello and Carlos Andrés Pérez, and more recently, in the investigations into the financing of Samper's election campaign). Nonetheless, these public scandals do not appear to represent the systematic enforcement of the law and judicial scrutiny over public posts. In effect, they are sometimes resolved by finding scapegoats for a brief period until the problem disappears.

Inadequate Infrastructure and Scarcity of Resources

In many countries in Latin America the judiciaries do not have adequate budgets, which keeps them from meeting even the most basic needs, so as to be able to guarantee access to justice for the public at large. Inadequate budgets perpetuate the dependency of the judiciary, generate corruption among court personnel, and impede the judiciary from attracting well-trained judges and support staff. The judiciary should have a separate budget that it controls, prepares, and submits to the legislature. Nonetheless, the link between the resources available to the courts and the time taken for the disposition of cases has been very weak. Indeed, there is no evidence of a significant correlation between judicial efficiency (measured by case backlogs and time delays) and the size of the government budget allocated to the courts.[12]

Two reasons for the lack of correlation are as follows: (i) the additional resources (staff and funds), which represent a semi-fixed cost for society, may initially reduce the backlog of cases and the delays, with improvements in the productivity of the courts, until the economic growth and added business activity impose new demands on the courts; and (ii) a judiciary with additional resources (for example, new buildings, more staff, and equipment) will begin to attract citizens and firms that were once reluctant to use the courts because of previous delays and high costs of litigation. These two factors will tend to increase the average number of proceedings per court and to increase, once again, the time for the disposition of cases. Their joint effects make it difficult to determine the consequences of adding or subtracting resources without a clear forecast of the demand for judicial services and of the impact of additional economic activity on the judiciary. Therefore, it is much more sensible to apply a budgetary mechanism in which the courts can request funds based on the anticipated increases in the number of proceedings in each specific area of the law and in each geographic jurisdiction.

Access to Justice

A fourth factor that hinders the capacity of the state to reform the judiciary stems from the problem of geographic distance, which is associated with the structural incapacity of the public sector to exercise authority and ensure respect for the law throughout the national territory and in its own courts. This is especially true of rural communities, isolated from the main trends in modernization. In order to foster an effective judiciary, the courts' supply of services must be met by a de-

---

[12] See Jesse Cassaus (1994).

mand for judicial services by the citizens who are willing to accept court proce-dures and the judges' final decisions. The absence of popular pressure for judicial reform, observed throughout Latin America, may be explained by the fact that in many cases the courts have become irrelevant to conflict resolution. For exam-ple, the peasants from the most remote rural regions of Peru would need to travel an average of 53.1 kilometers to reach a court to solve a legal dispute.[13] If we add the problems related to language and cultural barriers, it is clear that it is highly likely that recourse to the formal channels of justice will be avoided. Moreover, it is precisely at this remote local level that the rule of law is most frequently undermined by the discretional practices of local judges, in which coercion by the strongest often prevails. Under these conditions, the rural communities are marginalized from modern urban life and removed from the supposed benefits of constitutional democracy and the rule of law.[14] In such a setting, the potential users of the courts are very distrustful of legal procedures, preferring to avoid them.

Related to the physical difficulties in gaining access to justice are the prob-lems of cultural and racial isolation, particularly where the socioeconomic differ-ences are greatest or where the social and racial divisions continue unresolved. In these cases, the public distrusts and avoids the formal justice system. As a result, the formal legal mechanisms coexist with informal alternative mechanisms of justice (sometimes in the form of the traditional customs and laws of a commu-nity). For example, in poor urban areas, such as the *favelas* of Brazil, or the *villas miseria* in Buenos Aires, different forms of community justice arise that have very weak links with the formal mechanisms of law and order.[15] Once again, this indicates the failure of the public sector to provide an equitable rule of law.

The socioeconomic barriers to gaining access to justice are not fully worked out even in the most developed democracies. Imperfect access to information and knowledge about legal and procedural rights, or simply the high direct and indirect costs of access to the courts, are simple barriers that impede their use. In the context of the harsh realities of the Latin American societies, it is even harder to come up with a quick solution to these problems. For example, based on broad

---

[13] During judicial crises in Argentina, Ecuador, and Venezuela, the public use of court services de-clined dramatically. Surveys in those countries indicate that the courts are not used as dispute resolution mechanisms. (Buscaglia and Dakolias 1995).

[14] Many academics provide descriptions of how the so-called "informal sector" grows in spheres where the formal laws and regulations are completely ignored in day-to-day life. This social denial occurs in places where the formal rules that have the seal-of-approval of the state do not reflect the values or codes of conduct followed by the average citizen. For more details, see Hernando De Soto (1989).

[15] See Hernando De Soto (1989), and Daniel Carbonetto, Jenny Hoyle, and Mario Tueros (1988).

samples of cases brought before the court of first instance, it has been shown that the statistical correlation between family income, on the one hand, and length of court procedures and costs of litigation, on the other, is significantly negative in Argentina, Ecuador, and Venezuela.[16] In other words, low-income families tend to experience longer delays and higher costs in labor and civil courts.

Vested Interests and Institutional Inertia

The main obstacles to an effective judicial reform in Latin America are the vested interests within the justice apparatus itself—interests that may be threatened by any profound change in the current system. In large part, success in implementing reforms depends on those who are responsible for effective law enforcement.

In the short run, one can anticipate resistance to judicial reforms at many levels within the judicial hierarchy. The reasons may vary considerably, making any effort to define how these interests operate problematic. For example, the judges from the Supreme Court normally resent it when they are excluded from the legislative process, and aren't even involved as advisers in the reform initiatives.[17] The reforms may also entail a loss of discretionary powers, an increase in the control measures, and even greater responsibility at any level of the judiciary, which will be met with considerable distrust by the judges, prosecutors, and staff affected. Finally, measures that establish a system of compensation based on personal merit, which did not exist before, will be held in contempt by private persons or groups who had benefitted precisely from a more political and clientelist system of compensation. The degree to which this internal resistance may "sabotage" the judicial reform effort may be considerable, and years of persistent political initiative may be needed to overcome it.

The perception is widespread in Latin America that courts are used by government officials as a mechanism for obtaining rents.[18] For example, as ex parte communication is allowed and is a common practice in most of the coun-

---

[16] Based on the information from 100 cases per jurisdiction in each country, it was possible to relate the procedural times and the costs of litigation, which reflect socioeconomic variables (Buscaglia and Ulen 1995; Buscaglia and Dakolias 1995).

[17] In the first effort to reform the Chilean judiciary in the early 1980s, the lack of active participation by the judges during the legislative debate clearly led to a total failure.

[18] Rent-seeking in the judicial system is basically a redistribution of the private sector to the courts, imposed, either as an explicit cost (remuneration or added court fees) or as an implicit or invisible cost (lost productive opportunities). In our case, rent-seeking activities are simple transfers of wealth from the private sectors to the courts. Surveys of users of the courts in Argentina, Chile, Brazil, and Venezuela show that a growing proportion of litigants were forced to provide "informal incentives" to court officers in order to speed up the handling of cases that would otherwise be pending for many more years.

tries of Latin America, judges can use a large part of the day in meetings with the attorneys and the parties, separately. Such communication creates incentives for corrupt behavior and lack of accountability in the courts. If the judicial sector and other members of the government use the courts for profit, then we should not be surprised to find members of the court and their assistants blocking the judicial reforms that bolster effectiveness. In this context, the court reforms that promote uniformity, transparency, and accountability in the law enforcement process would necessarily diminish the ability of the courts to extract rents.

Previous studies have argued that the inertia of the judiciary stems from the fact that the benefits expected from the reform, such as additional economic growth or new investment, are long-term by nature, and cannot be captured directly by the reformers nor by the population in the short term.[19] Furthermore, the main costs of the reform are short-term by nature and are perceived by the judges as the cause of a diminution in the flow of rents in their courts in the short term (explicit payments and other privileges). This asymmetry between short-term costs and long-term benefits tends to block judicial reforms and explains why the reforms of the court, which would eventually benefit most segments of society, often face resistance and delays. In this context, to pull together a powerful coalition to support the reform, the sequence of reforms should ensure that the short-term benefits compensate the loss of rents experienced, in the short term, by the judicial officers in charge of implementing the changes. In other words, the initial reforms should be those that make it possible for some immediate benefits to flow into the hands of judicial officers, in an effort to compensate the short-term losses in their ability to garner bribes. In contrast, the proposed court reforms that generate long-term benefits to the judiciary need to be applied in the stages following the reform process.

During a profound crisis in the judicial system, the high costs imposed on the courts due to delays, backlogs, and informal incentives (which the public needs to supply to obtain the services of court officials) requires companies and citizens to reduce their demand for judicial services. The increase in the levels of bribes and rent-seeking by the courts also drives up the cost of access to justice. Therefore, a judicial crisis begins the moment that the backlogs, delays, and extraofficial payments drive up the costs (implicit or explicit) of access to the system. When the costs become sufficiently high, the population will limit the use of the judiciary to the point that the ability of the courts to secure rents will diminish.[20] When this point is reached, it is more likely that judicial reform will be ac-

---

[19] See Edgardo Buscaglia (1992b).
[20] A profound crisis is characterized by symptoms that range from unprecedented backlogs to unsustainable delays in the procedures. This situation reduces the demand for judicial services.

cepted by the members of the courts, in particular, and by the governments, in general, as a way to regain prestige and their ability to make their activity "profitable."[21] During a crisis, both court officers and politicians tend to lose the ability to extract rents from their public posts. Consequently, the price paid by the politicians and court officers for joining a judicial reform diminishes during a crisis. Thus, the judiciary will likely be more willing to carry out a thoroughgoing reform of the courts during a crisis, so long as the proposals for reform bring high short-term benefits, such as an increase in the administrative power of the courts of first instance, judicial independence, and an increase in the resources allocated to the courts.

This analytical framework explains why all the countries of Latin America that have progressed in judicial reforms first had to undergo a profound crisis with the characteristics mentioned above (i.e. an acute overall decline in the average number of proceedings filed for each of the civil courts), as in Argentina, Chile, Colombia, Costa Rica, Ecuador, and Venezuela. In these cases, additional short-term benefits were needed to ensure the political support of key judges, who were willing to discuss the judicial reform proposals only after a profound crisis diminished their ability to serve the public.[22] These benefits included generous early retirement packages, promotions for judges and their support staff, new buildings, and an expanded budget.[23]

Nonetheless, to ensure a lasting reform, the short-term benefits need to be channeled through institutional mechanisms, in which the likelihood the political directives will be revoked is very low. The best institutional scenario, one which would make it difficult to return to the previous state of affairs, is one in which the judicial reforms are the result of a consensus that involves the judiciary and at least one of the other two branches of government. Under such conditions, the coalitions needed for the change may exist only if the identities of many of the beneficiaries of the judicial reform are known by those who have decision-making capacity in the judiciary, the executive, and the legislature, prior to implementing that phase. A further condition is that the political influence of those who hope to benefit must counter the activities of the personnel who will lose their privileges, or who still depend on the exploitation of their public post.[24]

---

[21] Our empirical observations confirm that as backlogs and delays mount, the number of proceedings filed in each court tends to diminish.

[22] During a two-year reform period, Chile and Venezuela experienced increases of 56 percent and 75 percent, respectively, in real spending earmarked to the judiciaries (Buscaglia and Dakolias, 1995).

[23] See Buscaglia and Dakolias (1995) and Correa Sutil (1993).

[24] This assumes that the judicial reform also produces losers, however great the net gains may be.

Conclusion

In summary, there are always two opposing forces that explain why the governments of Latin America has failed to provide a judicial sector capable of strengthening democratic institutions and market economies.[25] First, an institutional change that increases efficiency, guided by the four principles developed above, can only partially explain the institutional transformation observed in the recent judicial reforms. Second, the government's ability to extract rents also accounts for some of the inertia observed, or the lack of institutional change. In brief, the nature of the relations among a society, its legal rules, and its judicial sector can be explained in terms of the political activities and arguments on economic efficiency. These two influences can also help shed light on the judicial and legal development of a nation.

A more effective court system, together with alternative dispute resolution mechanisms, supplied by the private sector, may foster the much-needed balance between equity and efficiency in the exercise of justice. This balance is not found anywhere in Latin America at this time. Indeed, there is a general lack of access to justice by the low-income sectors of the population. These barriers are due to the delays, backlogs, and widespread corruption in the courts. Only thorough judicial reform will reduce these barriers, and help to ensure the stability of democracy in Latin America.

---

[25] These considerations are crucial for understanding the failure of many market reforms. See Edgardo Buscaglia (1992a, 1995).

References

Buscaglia, E. 1995. Stark Picture of Justice in Latin America. *The Financial Times*, March 13, 1995.

———. 1992a. Now that Argentina's Stable, It's Time for a Revolution. *The Wall Street Journal*, August 28, 1992.

———. 1992b. Delineation of Property Rights and Economic Growth. Papers in Law and Economics. Berkeley: University of California.

Buscaglia, E. and Dakolias, M. 1995. Judicial Reform in Latin America: Economic Efficiency vs. Institutional Inertia. Working Paper Series No. 2367. Washington, D.C.: Georgetown University.

Buscaglia, E. and Ulen, T. 1995. A Quantitative Analysis of the Judicial Sectors in Latin America. Paper presented at the annual meeting of the American Law and Economics Association, May 12-13, 1995.

Carbonetto, D., Hoyle, J., and Tueros, M. 1988. *Sector informal*. Lima: Centro de Estudios para el Desarrollo y la Participación.

Cassaus, J. 1994. Court Administration in Latin America. Mimeo.

CIA. 1994. *CIA World Factbook*. Washington, D.C.: Central Intelligence Agency.

Correa Sutil, J. 1993. The Judiciary and the Political System in Chile: The Dilemmas of Judicial Independence During the Transition to Democracy. In Slotsky, Irwin, ed., *Transition to Democracy in Latin America: The Role of the Judiciary*. Boulder: Westview Press.

Correa Sutil, J. 1992. Diagnósticos acerca del sistema judicial chileno. In Guillermo Martínez, ed., *Justicia y libertad en Chile*. Santiago, Chile: Corporación LIBERTAS.

De Soto, H. 1989. *The Other Path: The Invisible Revolution in the Third World*. New York: Harper and Row.

O'Donnell, G. 1993. On the State, Democratization, and Some Conceptual Problems. Working Paper. Kellogg Institute, University of Notre Dame, Indiana.

Salas, L., and Rico, J. 1993. *Administration of Justice in Latin America*. Miami: International University Press.

World Competitiveness Report. 1994. Baltimore: Johns Hopkins University Press.

CHAPTER 3

Judicial Systems and
National Economic Performance

Robert Sherwood

Introduction

That institutions matter in important ways for national economic performance is apparent from common sense, and also from a growing body of research.[1] This is particularly evident in countries that have shifted from closed, state-dominated economic systems to market-oriented systems where private parties are expected to lead in making economic decisions.

As more countries adopt open-market economies and as the state withdraws from ownership and command, the role of the private sector gains importance. In this setting, how judicial systems function is increasingly relevant to private activity. Yet the link between the functioning of judicial systems and the performance of national economies has received little analysis.[2]

Among a nation's institutional arrangements, judicial systems provide a foundation on which other components depend. How the judiciary functions has a powerful influence on the economic decision-making of private parties. This influence is felt immediately by those who end up in court as litigants, whose immediate interests are affected. But others outside the process also learn what might happen if they engage in litigation. Few enter the courts, but many watch and make decisions based on what they see.

Many elements of a modern economy, such as bankruptcy law, collateral-based lending, public utility regulation, high-level technological research, and capital markets, rely on well-functioning courts. This reliance is often taken for granted, but little examined, by American and European researchers who study developing economies.

To frame the issue in numerical terms, consider how much a poorly functioning judicial system constrains the economic performance of a country. In oth-

---

[1] See, for example, Keefer and Knack (1994).
[2] See Weder (1995).

er words, if a country were likely to grow at an annual rate of about 3 percent, would the rate fall to 2.6 percent if its judicial system functions poorly? Some economists have analyzed certain Latin American economies together with aspects of their judicial systems' performance. Their results suggest that a poorly functioning judiciary may reduce growth by up to 15 percent, although others have estimated less.

Determining the effects of the judicial system on growth would suggest, at least approximately, the relative role of the judicial system compared with other institutional factors. The public needs a strong rationale to understand that judicial system reform should be a high priority. For example, just as the ministers of finance receive demands for budgetary resources to improve public health, education, and transportation, greater budgetary allocations should also be sought to reform the justice system. What is needed are solid indicators that show that an efficient and effective judicial system is an essential requirement for economic development.[3]

A deeper look at the issue might also help us to determine which corrections in our judicial systems would produce the largest impact on national economic performance.[4] For example, under a fully effective judicial system, resolving private contract disputes might influence overall economic activity less than would, say, improved judicial treatment of cases in which private parties assert their rights against government officials who have abused their discretion. Alternatively, the ability of private parties to challenge defective legislation might have the most sustained and positive influence on general economic conditions.

A Hypothetical Example

Suppose that three young engineers are forming a company to produce "Z-widgets," a product new to their country, which is stronger and less expensive than the closest comparable product. They have designed most of the product, but need to license a small package of related technology from a German company. They are concerned about whether their Z-widget will comply with an environmental protection law currently under debate in the national congress. The market for their product is confined largely to a major state-owned public utility. The press is reporting that in the aftermath of the recent elections, the new congressional leadership has threatened to privatize the utility in spite of a constitutional prohibition.

---

[3] This does not mean that merely increasing available funds will cure inefficiencies of the judicial system.

[4] The need for judicial system reform extends to the United States, where national economic performance has probably been impaired by a lack of certain reforms.

You can spot the issues that the engineers must ponder. If the judicial system in their country functions well, the German company will be more inclined to do business with them and may even offer terms that are more favorable than would be the case if the judicial system cannot be relied upon. Likewise, they would probably have some confidence that national financial institutions will be prepared to offer them funds for their project.

As to the environmental question, the outcome of the pending legislative debate may not be known for months, yet they want to decide now whether to press ahead. The fact that the courts are likely to give them a prompt, fair and reasonable decision if a dispute with a ministry official arises under the future law will encourage them to go ahead rather than drop their plans.

The status of their market potential is also affirmed by the presence of a judiciary which, under our assumptions, is ready to uphold constitutional standards against any unfounded legislative attack and ready to assure fair dealing by the utility.

Other Examples

Some informal examples may further illustrate the influence of judicial systems on economic activity:

- A striking example comes from Kenya, whose government once introduced a duty draw-back scheme intended to promote local employment and increase exports. The law was clearly written, but export companies found that ministry officials refused to make the payments authorized by the statute. Recourse to the judicial system followed, but the courts refused to act. As a result, the duty draw-back scheme was abandoned by private interests.
- In Bangladesh, commercial lending virtually collapsed after multiple litigants found the courts unwilling to enforce defaulted commercial loans. Apparently more than a few international companies left the country.
- In many Latin American countries, courts will act swiftly and decisively when personal checks are not supported by sufficient funds. As a result, personal checks are widely used for many transactions.
- In São Paulo, taxi drivers now insist that their passengers fasten their seat belts. Vigorous judicial enforcement of the new seat belt rule in a few well publicized cases brought about this startling change.
- The return of Hong Kong to China in 1997 presents a fascinating situation for study. Recently the future of Hong Kong's judicial system was decided. Appeal to British courts will end, with disputed cases to be sent to Beijing. How Hong Kong's judicial system will change as a result suggests an opportunity for further research on the judiciary's influence on economic activity.

Measuring Economic Impact

With cases like these multiplied across the economic landscape, what is the aggregate effect of a poorly functioning judicial system on one country's economic performance? We must wonder how much burden is placed on a national economy by the added expense of red tape, and how many times people decide to nothing at all. But it is difficult to measure increased transactions costs and far more difficult to measure what does not happen. Increased transactions costs and opportunity losses may impose heavy constraints on a national economy, yet there has been little attempt to measure either.

The study by Sherwood et al. (1994) raises the issue of measuring economic performance from the perspective of judicial system functioning. A judicial system influences private economic decision-making in at least six areas:

- private contractual practices
- creation and security of private property rights
- private party disputes with public administrators
- challenges to the quality of legislative enactments
- suppression of criminal activity
- credibility of public policy.

It should be possible to isolate and measure the ways that judicial system performance affects economic activity in each area. The following are some preliminary considerations.

Private Contractual Practices

Very limited research suggests that, in an economy with poorly functioning courts, private parties may resort to contractual practices which are less than efficient. For example, vendors may limit the quantities they are willing to sell on credit because of collection difficulties. Thus, economies of scale suffer. Contracting may be confined within social circles or family groups, making entry for outsiders difficult. This represses the division of labor that is at the heart of efficient modern economies. The size of firms may be larger than optimal because, to avoid contract enforcement difficulties, owners elect to produce components within their companies rather than source them from outside suppliers.

Creation and Security of Private Property Rights

Common sense alone tells us that if private property cannot be defended effectively in the courts, there will be a reluctance to acquire property which is otherwise vulnerable to loss. For example, if courts will not effectively defend owners against invasion of their land, owners are put to the expense of employing non-judicial means to defend against invasions. If copyright, patent and trademark infringements cannot be readily defeated in the courts, few will eagerly invest in the creation, acquisition and exploitation of intellectual property, and this reduces the technological base of the economy.

Private Party Disputes with Public Administrators

Public officials are wisely given authority to exercise discretion in executing their responsibilities as public administrators. Without the presence of courts which are willing and able to discipline officials who abuse their discretion, private activity which depends on discretionary approvals will tend to limit resource commitments or turn to inappropriate means to secure approvals. The duty drawback scheme in Kenya mentioned above illustrates the economic impact of this quite well. Future regulation of the many recently privatized state enterprises throughout Latin America will fit this category also.

Challenges to the Quality of Legislative Enactments

Where judges are able to render decisions which are critical of the quality of legislative enactments, a quiet discipline is asserted on those who prepare legislation and accompanying rules and regulations. In countries with effective judicial systems, congressional staff members work under the influence of their awareness that their legislative draftsmanship may come under judicial scrutiny. As a result, their work product is less likely to be sloppy and in conflict with other laws and rules, less likely to contradict constitutional mandates and less likely to require litigation to repair its defects.

Suppression of Criminal Activity

Recent research in Colombia has shown a correlation between the failure there to suppress criminal activity and declining national economic performance. Correlations are not the same as causes, but the data are striking. The abject failure of the judicial system in Colombia to deal with criminal activity surely reflects the horrendous conditions there stemming in large part from the narcotics trade. The wider economic consequence may well be that, by extension, general public confidence in the judicial system's ability to effectively deal with non-criminal matters is considerably reduced.

Credibility of Public Policy

A recent and continuing line of research[5] suggests that the credibility of economic policy may be even more important than its correctness. Only as credibility is assured are private investors willing to fully commit resources. These researchers report that judicial system effectiveness played an important but unmeasured role in assuring policy credibility: where people believed the courts would hold governments to their legally binding commitments, they were more willing to act in reliance on policy enactments. This in turn serves to release more private resources into the national economy, thereby stimulating sustained economic growth.

Conclusion

Finding appropriate methods to measure the economic performance of judicial systems is not easy. Even those who have worked in inefficient judicial systems can contribute little on this issue (Sherwood et al. 1994). One can perhaps identify cases where the judicial system has already experienced a change—Hong Kong is a good example—and compare the economic conduct of the factors "before and after" the change. It is also feasible to evaluate the impact of judicial reform on economic performance through a questionnaire survey of people who have worked in both systems.

Other ways of measuring the economic impact of judicial systems are being tried. IDESP, an independent study center in Sao Paulo, Brazil, with funding from the Tinker Foundation, recently undertook such measurements in examining tax, labor and commercial litigation.

Economists who have the requisite background to investigate this issue appear to be in short supply, however. Some knowledge of judicial systems is necessary, together with a capacity for research in institutional economics and experience with developing countries.

In this Hemisphere, as elsewhere, reform efforts based on ethics, morality or human rights have made limited progress. Recent reform efforts in the region are proceeding cautiously from the awareness that "something must be done," but, for the most part, they lack an articulated economic rationale. Almost certainly, deep-seated resistance to these reform efforts lies ahead, with a few early manifestations already reported. A potent economic rationale to help sustain these efforts and overcome resistance would be timely.

---

[5] See Borner, Brunetti and Weder (1995) and Brunetti and Weder (1992).

References

Borner, S., A. Brunetti, and B. Weder. 1995. *Political Credibility and Economic Development*. London: MacMillan.

Brunetti, A. and B. Weder. 1992. *Political credibility and economic growth*. WWZ-Studie Nr. 39, Wirtschaftswissen-schaftliches Zentrum der Universitat Basel. (September).

Keefer, P. and S. Knack. 1994. Institutions and Economic Performance: Cross-Country Tests Using Alternative Institutional Measures. IRIS Working Paper No. 109. College Park: University of Maryland, Center for Institutional Reform and the Informal Sector (IRIS).

Sherwood, R., G. Shepherd, and C. de Souza. 1994. Judicial Systems and Economic Performance. *Quarterly Review of Economics and Finance* 34 (Special issue, summer).

Weder, B. 1995. Legal Systems and Economic Performance: The Empirical Evidence. In *Judicial Reform in Latin America and the Caribbean*, edited by Malcolm Rowat, Waleed H. Malik and Maria Dakolias, World Bank Technical Paper Number 280. Washington, D.C.: World Bank.

CHAPTER 4

Lessons from the Political Economy of Other Reforms

Ricardo Hausmann

With the process of economic reforms embarked upon in the late 1980s, Latin American societies are learning in practice how fundamental the judiciary is to the development process. If the "market" is understood broadly as the place where property titles are exchanged, then its activities are defined by the legal framework and protected by the judicial system. With the growing complexity of contracts and trade, there is more need than ever for adequate forums to settle disputes among economic actors, whether labor-related, commercial, or financial. In addition, the most fundamental incentives for individual effort and savings depend on the security of person and property. Consequently, there are direct links between the justice system and economic development.

Although several countries have considered major reforms of their judicial systems, in practice few advances have been observed. Why, in a sector so important to society, have reform efforts been frustrated, in contrast to other areas?

The Political Economy of Judicial Reform

Part of the explanation is surely to be found in what we term the political economy of judicial reform. One way to understand this is by establishing parallels with other reforms under way in Latin America. This chapter will contrast the reform of the judicial system with the process of stabilization, trade liberalization, social security reform, and education reform. We will pose five questions regarding judicial reform, in order to determine factors that may accelerate its implementation and contribute to its success:

- Is there major dissatisfaction with the current situation?
- Is there an alternative solution to the problem?
- Does the reform face major opposition by pressure groups?
- Does the reform generate tangible, short-term benefits for sectors of society decisive to its implementation?
- Are there mechanisms to compensate those who are negatively affected by the changes?

Dissatisfaction with the Current Situation

To answer the first question, consider the experience of the stabilization process. Here the answer depends on the degree of inflation and society's tolerance. When inflation reaches 3 percent in Germany, or 30 percent in Colombia, it becomes a serious problem that must be solved. Nonetheless, in another country inflation might reach 70 percent without engendering much interest in making sacrifices to correct the situation.

This suggests that stabilization is only possible insofar as society is unwilling to tolerate more inflation, and is ready to assume the cost of bringing it down. Domingo Cavallo, formerly Argentina's minister of the economy, has remarked that the reforms implemented in his country would have been impossible at an earlier time. Not until they were faced with the devastating costs of hyperinflation were Argentines willing to make the sacrifices necessary to avoid it.

In contrast to those reforms aimed at stabilizing the economy, trade liberalization has seldom been viewed as an urgent task; the general opinion is that delays in its approval do not entail high short-term costs. Nonetheless, political support for trade reforms materialized only after a long period of mediocre growth, which gradually wore away at the bases of support for the previous trade protection regime.

In matters of social security, changes often take place after the system has already collapsed. Here reform appears as the only possible course of action, and so can be delayed no longer.

Reform of the education system, while by consensus one of the most important reforms in any development agenda, does not carry the urgency characteristic of other reforms. The education sector reflects reforms over the long term; more than a decade could pass before seeing substantial results of decisions made today. The quality of education is very difficult to measure, and how well it meets the needs of the economy can only be ascertained after new graduates enter the labor market. This lack of urgency and of signs of progress may help to explain the limited advances in this area.

In my view, judicial reform must contend with this same dynamic. All recognize that having an efficient judicial system is crucial for a country's development, but achieving it takes time, and the benefits are neither immediate nor easily observable. Moreover, society has a certain level of tolerance and a capacity to adapt to the current situation, which make reforms all the more distant.

The major challenge is to break with this dynamic, to keep judicial reform on the country's political agenda, and put in place incentives to implement and sustain it. To this end, society should understand the need for judicial reform and the costs of postponing it. Making more information available on the quality of judicial services may set off much-needed alarms to get society to respond. National education exams in some countries of the region have provoked major social reactions to the unsatisfactory performance of the educational system. A similar strategy might work in the case of judicial reform.

An Alternative Model

When an alternative model is available to solve a problem, reforms are facilitated. In seeking to stabilize inflation, for example, there is some agreement on the measures needed, which tend to reflect economic thinking in vogue at the time. In the late 1970s and early 1980s the *tablita* was used in Argentina. Then came more heterodox programs with the cruzado and the austral, and the 1985 stabilization program in Israel. Some countries, such as Bolivia (1985), Venezuela (1989), and Peru (1990), tried shock programs with a floating exchange rate. More recent are programs based on thoroughgoing monetary reforms, such as the *caja de conversión* in Argentina and the Real Plan in Brazil. While not all of them led to success, in each case there was a strategy deemed adequate to address the problem.

To take another example, trade liberalization has very simple guidelines. Basically, it requires that the government stop doing things it had been doing. For example, barriers to imports need to eliminated, high tariffs must no longer be charged, and so on. The model is simple and the pace of liberalization can be adjusted to address various technical or policy problems. Many countries have successfully liberalized their trade, so there are many models to follow.

The situation is somewhat analogous with reform of the social security system, which involves moving from a regime of distribution to one of individual capitalization. Chile's experience has become a guidepost for understanding what this entails and how it works. The model exists and is quite clear. Its implementation is all the more difficult the more mature the previous regime, and the more advanced the demographic transition. For example, Argentina's reforms should have been more modest, because the distribution system was already transferring 12 percent of GDP to pensioners, in contrast with 4 percent in Chile. Uruguay, Latin America's "oldest" country, has a pension burden that amounts to 17 percent of GDP. Thus recently adopted reforms accord less of a role to individual capitalization, as taxes on active workers are needed to pay retirees' pensions. There is little room for each to save for his or her own old age. This provides a clear incentive for reforming the social security system: the longer it takes, the more difficult it will be to implement.

The education sector, by contrast, has no clearly defined alternative model for reforms. The quality of education is very difficult to measure, which is a hindrance to defining what systems work better and what changes improve performance. Opinions regarding this diverge sharply: some propose standardized national exams because they would yield measurable results, making it possible to

introduce adjustments in the incentives system, in training educators, or in organizing the sector, and to verify whether they improve performance. Others consider this unnecessary meddling. Some suggest that highly centralized systems
become unmanageable and limit administrative capacity in individual schools.
Others fear that the lack of strong central control may lead to growing inequalities.

Nor is there a model to guide reform of judicial systems. The only model
available is the one already in operation, and reform is perceived as a leap into a
void, without persuasive evidence that change will improve matters. The bias
toward the status quo can only be turned around when dissatisfaction reaches
critical levels. Of course, one can establish a lengthy list setting forth what should
be addressed. For example, the reform should change the operation of the courts,
amend the constitution, expand the human resources allotted to each court, com-
puterize the handling of information, change procedures, and many other things
along these lines that are easily overlooked.

Without a concise analysis of what is wrong, it is difficult to communicate
with the public about what must be achieved, which is key for securing political
support and for sustaining the changes over time. This leads directly to the issue
of opposition groups that may affect implementation of the reform.

Opponents to Reform

In general, the more refined the framework for reforms, the easier it is to identify
groups that will oppose them. If stabilization requires a major monetary adjustment, and that major adjustment entails an increase in interest rates, opposition
will come from industry, agriculture, and mortgage loan holders. The natural enemies of trade liberalization are the sectors protected by current policy. In the
case of social security, if the reform entails a reduction in benefits, such as increasing the retirement age from 60 to 65 years, then groups in certain age brack-
ets are more affected. Once we have a clear understanding of the measures to be
adopted, we can anticipate and better gauge the degree of opposition to expect.

In this regard, education reform is particularly traumatic. This kind of reform requires transforming the bureaucracy that provides the service; in this process groups form as they feel threatened by the changes to be implemented. For
example, teachers' unions, who sit opposite the government in the negotiations,
generally oppose plans to improve measurements of the quality of education and
mechanisms used to supervise the quality of teaching staff.

When analyzing the judicial system, it is important to bear in mind that its
reform also involves transforming the bureaucracy that provides the service. Those
with vested interests in the bureaucracy may become an obstacle to reform, rather than an element supporting it.

Beneficiaries of Reforms

If reforms yield short-term benefits, this may cushion the opposition, or create support groups outside the sector. That is the fourth question: Does the reform generate immediate benefits for groups who are crucial to its implementation?

In the case of inflation, the answer is yes. The episodes of stabilization were followed by economic booms, a major expansion of consumption, and a decline in unemployment. Consequently, reforms that were at first unpopular received more support as they scored successes. This swift materialization of benefits can muster a political base to sustain reforms.

Identifying tangible short-term benefits and forming support groups are not features of trade liberalization, however. Consumers, who constitute a very large group, are the principal beneficiaries of the wider array of goods that liberalization makes possible. Nonetheless, consumers as a group rarely exercise much political pressure. This atomization of beneficiaries, in contrast to the greater extent of organization of the persons affected, means that while a trade opening may yield some short-term benefits, the recipients don't necessarily organize to offer political support. This is one of the reasons why trade liberalization is never proposed in isolation, but is included as part of an overall reform program. A negotiation ensues in "take it or leave it" terms, it is likely that people will raise less opposition to this particular point, because they want other aspects of the reform package to move forward.

In the area of social security, management of pension funds appears to be an excellent business opportunity, especially for groups in the financial system. While this can produce immediate support for the reform, it may also lead to resentment if workers fail to see how they stand to benefit under the new regime. It may appear to them that the only ones who will gain from pension reform are the bankers supporting it.

Regarding reform of the judicial system, the benefits are neither so evident nor so short-term. While there is dissatisfaction with the system's general operation, it is unclear what aspects will improve first, and how they will affect various groups. The lack of clear objectives for the reform in terms of measurable results makes it difficult to perceive its benefits. In addition, many people only use the judicial system occasionally. If reform is a trial-and-error process, it may delay tangible benefits for those groups whose political support is decisive.

Compensating Losers

Is it possible to design a reform that compensates the losers? If a country can achieve a stable economy without generating a short-term recession, this increases the viability of the stabilization policies. In trade liberalization, it is difficult to compensate the losers. The liberalization process often begins with a major devaluation, so as to cushion its impact in the initial phases. This happened in many countries of the region, including Colombia, Ecuador, and Venezuela: although trade liberalization was expected to face major opposition, it did not materialize.

In relation to social security, it is feasible to design the reform so as to try to compensate the losers. For example, the workers may be given the option of sticking with the current regime, or joining the new arrangement. Another possibility is to offer them bonds recognizing their acquired rights under the old system. Both approaches increase the costs associated with the reform, but make it politically viable.

The key to winning support for the education reform is to negotiate a salary increase in exchange for altering teachers' work regimes, as Mexico did in 1993 and Bolivia in 1995. In the various judicial systems, many of which lack sufficient resources, something similar could be considered. For example, increased resources for infrastructure or salaries could be offered in exchange for certain organizational changes.

However, if budget increases are not accompanied by the reforms negotiated, they result in the same judicial system, at a greater cost. If negotiations fail the first time, there may not be a second time: it is difficult to win political support for a new reform effort after a failed attempt with major social costs.

Elements for Successful Judicial Reform

Certain elements could prove helpful in reforming judicial systems. First, if reform is to be successful, the public must develop a keen sense of dissatisfaction with the status quo. This dissatisfaction may be related to impunity, with how the system handles the population locked up in pretrial detention, or with the other costs and hindrances to trade caused by an ineffective judicial system.

Second, the principles of the reform must be integrated. At present, there is no such synthesis, but rather a long list of parts of the system that need to be transformed. The first priority is to put the major ideas of the reform into focus.

Third, we know that the reform has few natural opponents in the public at large. Everyone prefers better justice than worse justice. The problems arise, as in education, in the course of negotiating with the director producers of the service, be they employees of the judicial system or the attorneys who litigate.

The incentives structure of the current regime is especially perverse, in both education and justice. For example, the school budgets are paid for indirectly, independent of the number of children who attend or their academic performance. The budget of the courts is covered, and is independent of the number of cases processed, or other efficiency indicators. Changing the incentives structure would have the resources follow the products of the system, not the costs, and give the users the power to choose among alternative suppliers, with budgetary resources following their decision.

Much could be gained by attempting to implement such changes. Nonetheless, existing problems need to be gauged objectively, in order to verify the success of the first steps and maintain support for the process. If the additional economic incentives proposed for those providing the service today are bearing fruit, that will help to secure support for continuing the reform.

The process of transforming the judicial system poses many challenges of a political nature. Trade liberalization, by contrast, requires only a presidential decree. And when inflation is reduced, results can be observed in the short term, so that the public feels more connected to the reform.

Of course, those most involved in the judicial sector will be very keen to observe what is happening and to understand the measures that have been adopted. But the public and the political system may remain relatively unaffected by these advances.

Since judicial reform must address this context, some points merit special attention. First, performance measurements are needed for the sector that reflect changes in productivity, and in the quantity and quality of the service provided. These indicators should made public, just as inflation and unemployment figures are published. One could show, for example, the number of persons locked up who have yet to be tried; the percentage of unsolved crimes; or the existing barriers to investment in sectors that require protection of intellectual property rights, such as the pharmaceutical industry, computer programs, and so on.

Second, special attention should be given to the incentives system introduced in the sector, which are a means to induce changes in conduct. Introducing incentives is not difficult in a market structure, such as the private market for lawyers. A lawyer with a good reputation can charge much higher rates, thereby creating incentives for lawyers to enhance their reputation, win cases, and so forth. But the remuneration paid to judges cannot be based on such criteria. In the judicial sector, in particular, incentives are aimed at developing a long-term judicial career. Nonetheless, insofar as the products of the system are measurable, the court can be paid based on output, rather than expenditures. This would establish incentives for efficiency, tying remuneration to performance. To rely solely on the promise of a stable and secure career, as is done today, cannot be the solution. Latin America's experience has shown that having efficient public administration and also a secure long-term career may be completely contradictory goals. Reconciling these two aspects is a great challenge that the judicial reform will have to address.

Third, if a society really wants to improve its judicial system, more budgetary resources are required, which entails some risks. When economists confront a problem, they ask: What incentives can be introduced to solve the problem?

When lawyers confront a problem, they ask: What law applies? In other words, there is a temptation to include in the Constitution, or in the laws, a provision by which the judiciary must receive one or two percent of the budget, which may further delay reforms.

The judicial system must demonstrate a legitimate need for additional resources. Some sectors seek to secure their legitimacy by appealing to the benefits they yield for society; this can become a vicious circle. A good example along these lines is, once again, the education reform. Society perceives that the quality of the service received is so low that it is not willing to increase the budget for education—because the public views this as squandering resources.

The judicial system has to gain legitimacy for a higher budget. Once the public understands that additional resources will mean improvements in a service that is fundamental to progress, it will be pleased to support and finance the transformations needed in the sector. The change in the amount of public financing should be accompanied by a reform in how these resources compensate the participants of the system, and by a change in how the system's performance is measured. Otherwise, it will be difficult to sustain judicial reform, which is one of the most complex and important reforms needed for Latin America's future development.

CHAPTER 5

Institutional Reliability
and Development

Rudolf Hommes

A transparent, reliable legal system, compatible with the customs of a country, is an essential requirement for developing trade systems that allow and encourage economic growth. Attaining this objective also requires a complex government structure capable of imposing and enforcing the law. The role of the state is to define and apply rules in a transparent and consistent fashion, and to provide efficient mechanisms for conflict resolution. This role facilitates impersonal trade and cuts transaction costs in the market.[1] In addition, the government and the political system should act to minimize violence and restrict the channels through which the wealthy can exercise influence.[2]

Insofar as these conditions are not obtained, a government lacks autonomy. If a government becomes vulnerable to pressures of force or money, it serves purposes foreign to public interest, loses its impartial status, and consequently is highly susceptible to corruption. In such conditions, government cannot be an agent of progress and facilitate economic growth.

On examining the legal systems of Latin America, the relationship between the state and the economic power, and the effectiveness of law enforcement, it is clear that much institutional development is still needed to attain a stable and reliable legal environment compatible with and capable of enforcing the law.

Lack of Transparency

The Italian Luigi Barzini (1985) described his country's legal system as follows:

> It has been proved that the laws, being so numerous, contradictory, and ambiguous, could allow a determined government to carry out any kind of revolution—of the extreme left or extreme right—by merely selecting a few

---

[1] See, for example, North (1987) and Buscaglia (1993).
[2] See Huntington (1968).

appropriate statutes and applying them to their ultimate consequences. No one knows how many laws are still valid, no one knows for certain what some of them really mean. Often, not even recourse to the records of what lawmakers said, years before, when debating them in Parliament, reveals their significance and precise purpose. A curious Italian superstition generates this continuous stream of laws: when things go wrong, problems are baffling, and nothing else avails, a new law is usually passed, often too difficult and complicated to be applied properly, in the hope that it will... act like an incantation and ward off that particular evil. Some, of course, are useful. A few are good. Many useless or impractical ones have been forgotten, "abrogated by desuetude" is the technical term; but all can be suddenly rescued from oblivion, dusted, and used at any time to benefit a powerful group, as weapons for the destruction of its enemies.

Courts do little to disentangle the confusion. Few Italians in their right mind expect anything but erratic justice from courts. The current rule is never to sue when one is in the right. It is too risky. One should go to court only when one is in the wrong and on the defensive.

This description of the Italian legal system can be applied, more or less, to the legal systems of several Latin American countries. An excess of legislation has created a legal morass that complicates court proceedings and decisions, so that the entire judicial system becomes erratic.

Lack of transparency is one reason for the uncertainty of legal systems, as rules proliferate and the resulting confusion give rise to creative interpretations and unpredictable court decisions. Another cause of the uncertainty is corruption, from which neither the region nor its courts are exempt.

Unpredictability

From an economic perspective, another factor that contributes significantly to uncertainty is the random and arbitrary nature of court decisions. This arbitrary action flourishes in legal environments plagued by a morass of regulations. If judges can be random and arbitrary, the legal system becomes a disincentive for private investment decisions, as it compounds economic uncertainty considerably.

Along the same lines, if judges' decisions are motivated by factors unrelated or adverse to economic growth, they tend to create institutions and rules that obstruct contractual relationships and the exercise of property rights. This in effect condemns the society to economic stagnation or decline. Judges in many Latin American countries fail to consider the economic consequences of their decisions. A legal system that does not understand or attribute importance to the economic effects of its conduct will not contribute to development, and is likely to promote institutions that will clash with economic development. In the best case, such a legal system will be mediocre in terms of economic efficiency, and its institutions will not contribute to economic progress.

In those countries where courts are informed of economic issues, and give serious consideration to the practical consequences of their decisions, economic development proceeds much more quickly. Such courts tend to encourage legal institutions that facilitate impersonal trade, a legal environment suited to more efficient performance of contracts, and a property rights regime more consonant with economic development.

Examples of the anti-economic direction of judicial decisions abound. The Colombian Constitution prohibits the state from granting assistance to private health care or education institutions, for example, but allows contracts with such institutions to carry out activities in the public interest, such as providing free or subsidized health care or education. Nonetheless, the Constitution also stipulates that such activities of public interest must be in accordance with the development plan approved by the Congress in 1991. That development plan was in limbo from 1991 to 1995, when it was finally "enacted." The Constitution did not provide for any temporary means to employ this plan during the four years after its promulgation, and the Colombian Council of State did not allow such services provision contracts to go forward. The result was that institutions that provide a significant part of the health services to the poorest part of the population did not receive state financing for four years, as the Council blocked all regulatory initiatives of the government during the transition period.

Regarding investment decisions, consider the consequences of the following events involving the privatization of a Colombian bank. The Constitutional Court decided that some sections of the law under which the privatization had been carried out were unconstitutional. But the Court failed to clarify that the privatization contracts that had been executed under the law were still valid; and the Court has established the doctrine that all acts entered into under a statute they later rule unconstitutional may subsequently be struck down. As a result, these privatization contracts have been litigated before the Council of State, whose record of decisions gives no hint as to the likely outcome, and whose caseload is so enormous that the decision may take several years. Those who acquired a bank under the law in force at this time run the risk of seeing the transaction voided at any time in the future. This is the coup de grâce for privatization processes from the courts, whether out of carelessness, negligence, or ideological considerations.

The procedures, decisions, and doctrines described are at the root of judicial insecurity in Colombia. Here respect for the letter of the law has prevailed over the spirit of the law, and innovative doctrines have been introduced without considering their economic consequences. It has gone so far that decisions are made "at law," with constitutionalist zeal, without taking account of the fact that the law is meaningless if applied outside a specific social context.

Economic Consequences of Activism

This kind of legal activism based purely on theory (in the void so attractive to Colombian judges) is also found in other countries of the region. When combined with populist political activism, it can lead to excesses. For example, in some countries the courts have adopted an anti-taxation position; in others they tend to decide on behalf of the pecuniary interests of regional and local governments to the detriment of the national treasury, without gauging the economic consequences of such decisions. This type of populist political activism goes much further than the liberal traditions of activism on behalf of fundamental rights, or underprivileged groups: it becomes a crusade against fiscal orthodoxy, or against a supposed economic centralism, and it may be a potent cause of economic instability.

In addition, it represents meddling by the courts in an area that is the exclusive domain of the executive and legislative branches. The central government can hardly be accountable for macroeconomic performance where courts are creating fiscal burdens for the sake of some advanced trend in constitutional interpretation, or in defense of the rights of the municipalities and regions. Moreover, by failing to consider the economic requirements of fiscal management, the judicial sector is usurping powers that belong exclusively to the congressional and executive branches of government.

Such conduct of the courts portends serious risks of economic instability. Contemporary economic literature indicates that budgetary institutions yield better fiscal results when Congress does not hold so much power, and when the Executive has veto power over the legislature.[3] Clearly, if the judiciary can make budgetary determinations yet not be held accountable, then the results will be worse than when Congress controls such decisions. When the courts act "at law," without pondering the economic effects of their decisions, then accountability vanishes, because they can assume they are defending a right without giving attention to the costs of that right to the treasury and to society. According to Alexander Bickel (1975):

> Few definite, comprehensive answers on matters of social and economic policy can be deduced from [the Constitution]. The judges, themselves ...removed from political institutions by several orders of magnitude, ought nev-

---

[3] A brief outline of the literature and empirical results that corroborate this idea can be found in Alesina, Hausmann, Hommes, and Stein (1995).

er to impose an answer on the society merely because it seems prudent and wise to them personally, or because they believe that an answer—always provisional—arrived at by the political institutions, is foolish. The Court's first obligation is to move cautiously, straining for decisions in small compass, more hesitant to deny principles held by some segments of the society than ready to affirm comprehensive ones for all, mindful of the dominant role the political institutions are allowed, and always anxious first to invent compromises and accommodations before declaring firm and unambiguous principles.

The need for courts to affirm certain principles is recognized, and some judicial activism leads to social and institutional change. But lack of accountability carries enormous risks: the economic risks of an activist court that ignores the practical consequences of its actions, and the political risks of a court that decides by deference to antipathies, prejudices, or personal intentions. Far better is the advice that Bickel attributes to Edmund Burke: "[The courts should] neither produce something completely new nor preserve something completely obsolete." At least not with respect to matters that affect macroeconomic stability or private investment.

Compliance with the Law

In order for laws and institutions to have the desired economic consequences, there must be a third party, the government, that is impartial, immune from violent or pecuniary pressures, and capable of enforcing the law and ensuring it meets with compliance.

Such a government is not to be found in any country of Latin America. In some countries, laws cannot be enforced because the army does not allow it; in others, the property and lives of citizens cannot be protected because the army has ceded large territories to guerrilla forces, which impose their own rules. In still others, bureaucratic or political elites place themselves above the law based on the hegemony of dominant parties. Thus the capacity of the state to uphold the law, to enforce contracts, and to defend property rights is severely limited in many parts of Latin America.

Moreover, there are powerful economic groups that exercise influence over government decisions to such an extent as to call into question their impartiality. This is more critical in some countries where economic power is not only in the hands of organizations engaged in lawful activities, but is also exercised openly by organized crime.

Conclusion

Despite a legal tradition that goes back several centuries, our judicial institutions and standards for enforcing the laws are far from achieving a minimum standard of economic efficiency. The legal systems of Latin America are excessively entangled, and hardly transparent. Arbitrary judicial decisions are all too common; and the political and economic activism of judges make it impossible to foresee the outcome of a proceeding. These conditions present obstacles to fair and open trade and the economic and technological development of society, which require clear and predictable judicial procedures, rules that favor property rights, the inviolability of contracts, and an independent state that can enforce these rules. At the present time in Latin America, legal proceedings and the resulting institutional framework tend to discourage rather than stimulate development.

References

Alesina, Alberto, Hausmann, Ricardo, Hommes, Rudolf, and Stein, Edward. 1995. "Budget Institutions and Fiscal Performance." Mimeo. Washington, D.C.: Inter-American Development Bank, Office of the Chief Economist.

Barzini, Luigi. 1985. *The Italians*. New York: Atheneum.

Bickel, Alexander. 1975. *The Morality of Consent*. New Haven: Yale University Press.

Buscaglia, Edgardo. 1993. *Law, Technological Progress and Economic Development*. Working Paper Series in Economic Development. Hoover Institute, Stanford University.

Huntington, Samuel. 1968. *Political Order in Changing Societies*. New Haven: Yale University Press.

North, Douglass. 1987. Institutions, Transaction Costs and Economic Growth. *Economic Inquiry* 25 (July).

CHAPTER 6

Democracy, Rule of Law, and Economic Efficiency

Tomás Liendo

Argentina's judicial reforms have been part of the ongoing process of institutional rebuilding, and our experience can serve to illustrate the importance of judicial institution to the public sector as a whole. Since 1983, Argentina has been restructuring its government institutions in accord with its Constitution. Since 1989, we have undertaken comprehensive economic reforms, aimed at narrowing the gap that separates us from the most developed countries.

Three principles—democracy, the rule of law, and economic efficiency—are paramount if these processes are to be sustained over time. The first, a democratic republic, is linked to separation of powers and respect for individual guarantees. It may happen, for example, that the popular sovereignty inherent in democratic government calls for adopting a given measure, whereas the basic institutions of the republic require that the decision be deferred, in view of long-term risks it could entail. For example, not even with a popular majority would it be lawful to undermine the separation of powers or guarantees of individual rights.

The separation of powers that is fundamental to our government can be viewed in terms of the institutional role of each branch. Those different branches have to work toward the same goal—the well-being of society as a whole. The functional division among branches prevents a situation in which all reins of power lie in the same hands, which could throw the balanced process off-track and distance it from the common good.

Each branch of government still has a responsibility to make appropriate decisions in any circumstances, but especially when dealing with matters pertaining to the common good. For example, the judiciary, in analyzing institutions or reform processes, economic or otherwise, cannot operate in the abstract, but must consider the objective consequences of their decisions.

That processes of change are led by majorities is an inherent principle of democratic government. Nonetheless, the responsibility of the majority in opting for change should include respect for minorities, be they social, ethnic, or political minorities. The challenge is to incorporate all elements and attend to the voices of minorities, which are helpful in attaining the overall objectives.

At the same time, citizens must rely on the national government to respect and protect their constitutional guarantees and rights, not only within the courts (which ultimately protect them), but also within the legislative and executive branches. What we term the rule of law, or the predictability of law, is a fundamental value of a democratic republic.

Of course the rule of law cannot be understood merely as a means of preserving the status quo. The status quo is sometimes altered to accord with fundamental values. We must do this with a revolutionary thrust in some cases, in order to set new institutions in motion that will accelerate the progress of our peoples.

In Argentina's case, economic reforms called for change in many institutions. We have abandoned price controls and exchange rate controls; we have also eliminated certain regulations that were impediments to economic activity. Consequently it was necessary to consolidate the internal debt, amend the legal regime governing the currency, and redefine relations with our creditors. These measures represented a break with the previous legal norms. Had we stuck with a formal conception of the rule of law, we would still be at the starting point (i.e., 1989). In effect, we would have placed at risk much more important values than the order that we had to leave behind.

For example, it was essential that Argentina restore its currency as the common denominator of economic transactions. Without such a common denominator, no contracts can be enforced, and all contracts are susceptible to lack of foreseeability, which introduces great uncertainty and has a damaging effect on the conduct of contracting parties. Therefore when introducing the monetary reform, we derogated all legal regulations—even those established by decision of two or more parties to a contract—that provided for indexing mechanisms, and prohibited any other form of indexing in the Argentine economy. Returning to a situation in which public and private contracts can be carried out with greater foreseeability has been crucial. So has the simplification of legal and regulatory provisions, with the essential objective of popularizing knowledge of the law.

As a widely accepted matter of principle, the law is presumed to be known. If ignorance of the law were a defense, it would be impossible to enforce the law. Still, not even specialists in our increasingly complex world have full knowledge of the contents of the law. Therefore, norms should be clear and simple to facilitate predictability and create public confidence in legal institutions.

In the past, much of Latin America's economic activity was subject to specific regulations, and the economies were relatively disconnected from the world's financial and capital markets. Various regulatory frameworks were imposed that were as artificial as they were supposedly supplementary. Price controls, export and import quotas, and manipulation of the exchange rate were culturally imposed policies.

Now, with the increasing integration of the world economy, deregulation also makes it possible to increase judicial security and legal certainty. Establishing a new economic and institutional order has become possible—an order that generates legal norms with lasting stability, preceded by periods in which the public is afforded an opportunity to adapt to the new context.

Of course, judicial security increases with the internal harmonization of a federal state, and external harmonization with other nations—or in the context of integrated markets, in an increasingly globalized world. Finally, consolidating the reform program also requires that a modern, efficient, and effective legal system be in place, with judges who receive ongoing training, and who employ basic and unalterable principles of equity in keeping with a standard of reasonableness.

CHAPTER 7

What to Expect of Judicial Reform

Santos Pastor

The purposes of judicial reform, as well as the anticipated results, are similar for many countries. This analysis will encompass the various costs and yields of reform, including its economic effects.[1] Certain practical measures are proposed for the reform of justice systems in general, which could substantially reduce the major problems suffered by the judiciary, and hence by society.[2] The proposed measures are grouped based on their impact on the supply and demand for judicial protection, in order to emphasize the incentives they can establish. After describing the measures, we review some of their costs and effects—both economic and non-economic, private and public—and their anticipated yield, both for losers and for those who will benefit.

This presentation is limited to the administration of justice and associated issues. Other aspects of the legal system that are key for economic development include defining property rights and liability rules. Likewise, establishing institutions that reduce transaction costs and deter unlawful activity are important dimensions of the legal system, but will be addressed only insofar as they relate to administrative systems.

General Aspects of Judicial Reform

To what extent is judicial reform necessary? The weakness of judicial institutions in many countries entails serious failures to protect rights, which inhibits socially useful action (such as investment and production), or causes conflict and waste of resources. Without independent, efficient, and competent justice, there are no secure guarantees for rights, and contracts are subject to uncertainty.

---

[1] The Council of Europe formed long-term working groups on the efficiency and equity of civil and criminal justice, whose results are applicable to other parts of the world (Council of Europe 1995). See also Santos Pastor (1993) and Richard Posner (1985).

[2] Each country has its own circumstances and problems that will require different policies, of course, even when the objectives are similar.

Because a reliable system of property rights and contracts is a necessary condition for fair transactions, the legal system must define and protect rights, and facilitate their exchange. The legal system thus has an importance much greater than its share of the government budget implies. Similarly, a bad legal system may be a serious dead weight to development efforts. Investors avoid countries where the basic foundations of law are fragile, because the legal system and the economic system are mutually dependent. The legal system plays a crucial role for the very existence of social life, and hence for economic development. On the other hand, economic development is a prerequisite for improving and sometimes even recognizing individual rights, not only economic rights.

Without an effective justice system, however, the anticipated value[3] of the legal system vanishes. The value of rights depends both on their contents and on their effective enforcement or protection, and to that end an effective judicial system is essential.[4]

What are the common problems of judicial systems in Latin America? Certain evils of greater or lesser intensity afflict the justice systems in many countries. Some of the most common are lack of independence vis-à-vis political authorities or pressure groups, the deficient quality of decisions (due to shortcomings in training or pressure brought to bear on judicial personnel), backlogs and delays, waste of available resources, and occasionally, lack of resources. These major problems are accompanied by more specific ones, which sometimes explain the major ones. For example, the excessive litigation that stems from traffic accidents is related to case backlog in the courts that settle such matters.

What is the aim of judicial reform? To achieve an independent, competent, and efficient judiciary branch, independent of the other branches of government, of pressure groups, and of all personal influence. Independence in performing its functions, however, does not mean lack of accountability. It must be competent, which requires training appropriate to the endeavors to be carried out in each sphere and level of decision-making. And it must be efficient, which means eliminating the waste of resources.

Nonetheless, the administration of justice is not an end in itself, but one means to ensure that rights are protected and rules observed. Society seeks the maximum protection of rights attainable at the least possible cost, and judicial protection is not the only way to achieve this. Some alternative mechanisms are

---

[3] The anticipated value of a remedy when rights are violated results from multiplying the value of that remedy by the probability that it is enforced. The probability can be interpreted generally as the frequency with which the remedy is enforced.

[4] As well as checks and balances among the various branches of government.

available for attaining these ends, whose relative virtue we should evaluate and contrast with the judicial option.[5]

Who should carry out the reform? The entire administration of justice, in its three basic dimensions: personnel, organizations, and rules. In effect, the reform should involve all the personnel, be they judges, clerks, officers, auxiliaries staff, or agents of the administration of justice; legal professionals (attorneys and expert witnesses); and parties to cases and users. Furthermore, it should extend to all the entities, from the judge's chambers to the governing bodies of the judiciary. Finally, the rules of procedure need to be amended[6] to bring them into line with current needs. They could be less permissive, for example, with delaying tactics.

What mechanisms can and should be used in the reform? In the general terms in which we are now speaking, there are two major sets of mechanisms: incentives to individuals and organizations, and supervisory and control mechanisms. All of these mechanisms require an appropriate information system on staff, results, and proceedings, which, in addition to being used for the management of the entire system, can also take stock of the work done.

Who will benefit or lose from reforms? Many of these specific measures will generate social well-being in net terms. Nonetheless, there will be strong resistance from certain groups of losers, especially those already organized in professional associations, such as trial judges. Except during major political changes, judicial reform tends to be an "enlightened" movement rather than a social movement. Unlike reform of pension systems, employment policy, or the struggle against crime, social dissatisfaction with the current situation is not immediate or intense. In general, judicial reform lacks a homogeneous and active social base capable of providing leadership in the hope of obtaining benefits greater than its costs.

What preparation is needed to solve specific problems? Any effort at substantial reform should begin with a sound identification and good sense of the specific problems faced, a reasonable explanation of the causes, anticipation of the consequences, and an assessment of the relative virtues of the various possible remedies. In practice, of course, decisions are often made in uncertain conditions and without adequate information. Even so, recognizing that these limitations exist, we have no better way to solve the problems of justice.[7] To carry out these tasks it is essential to draw on various social sciences, including economics.

---

[5] These are what have come to be known as alternative dispute resolution mechanisms—mediation, arbitration, conciliation, administrative proceedings, and even the liberalization of markets and access to information.

[6] This may also affect substantive rules.

[7] Judicial policy is a neglected area of public policy research.

Reforms Affecting the Supply of Judicial Protection

In modern administrative science, information systems are crucial both for management and for taking stock of outcomes. Activity indicators, for example, can be used to measure what is produced (judgments vs. decrees) in each jurisdiction and in each court, its quality[8] and duration, personnel and material resources of each court, costs of providing the public service, trends in decisions, and so forth.

Such information makes other evaluations possible. For example, evaluations based on output/input ratios, such as how many matters are settled or judgments handed down per trial judge or per person employed, determining the cost per case and quantifying the delay, all in a time or transversal (comparative) perspective. Then more complex evaluations regarding court efficiency can be made by analyzing residuals, by discriminant analysis,[9] or other procedures.[10]

The principal long-term guidelines for ensuring the supply of judicial protection, by producing more at less cost, should be the following: reform the incentives for judicial personnel, increase flexibility and decentralization, and improve organization at every link of the chain, from the courts of first instance to the Supreme Court, and from the halls of government of the various courts to the directing and general governing bodies in place (Ministry of Justice, Council of the Judiciary, or other).

In particular, it is very important to ensure efficient operation of the judicial chambers. Among other things, this requires that judges judge, not manage; that it be the judicial clerks or administrators with adequate training, who manage; and that mechanisms be put in place to allow for flexible management, making it possible to monitor and evaluate the results, and to provide incentives accordingly.[11]

What about more resources? In some countries the justice system suffers a dramatic scarcity of resources, either as a whole or, more commonly, in certain

---

[8] Among the quality indicators for judicial decisions are the ratio of judgments to appeals and the frequency with which initial judgments are overturned. Other indicators are the treatment accorded users, waiting times, or other facts. Combining objective information and opinion surveys can provide valuable indicators on the quality of service.

[9] Analysis of residuals typically uses regression techniques and interprets the positive or negative residuals from the various courts as indicators of good or bad results, respectively. Discriminant analysis builds a "frontier" of courts with the best results, and interprets and measures the results of the others based on their position with respect to the courts situated on that frontier. An interesting application of these techniques to the justice system can be seen in Francisco Pedraja and Javier Salinas (1995).

[10] One way to encourage empirical analysis of legal systems is to train researchers to use whatever statistical information is available.

[11] Some clerks may resist management tasks; others may charge that reforms represent "an attack on judicial independence," or find other objections, but these difficulties are not insurmountable.

quarters of the judiciary, and any measure to be taken must begin with more resources. But any reform that relies only or mainly on increasing the human, material, and financial resources will be misguided; there are already many examples of squandered resources. Sometimes, offering more protection only requires making better use of available resources.[12]

As a final note to this brief review of supply-side measures, I should emphasize the importance of each organization and even each individual having clearly assigned tasks. Objectives must be defined for each procedural stage that make it possible, first, for each person to do what is expected, and, second, to measure the degree to which the objectives sought are attained. Lack of definition, here as in other areas of public policy, is a source of inefficiency and arbitrary action.

What is the foreseeable impact of such reforms? Efficiency gains make it possible to provide more protection with a given amount of resources, or to spend less to attain a given level of judicial protection. In general, it will allow for a mix that consists of reducing delay, increasing access for cases that otherwise might not get a hearing, and improving the quality of performance. As noted above, these consequences are good not only for the judicial system itself, but for realizing rights and increasing economic transactions. Most reform policies, other than those that call for increased human and material resources, do not entail substantial public expenditure.

The legal personnel affected cannot be expected to support most of these policies. To begin with, the resistance to being evaluated or to having to account for the job done is notable at all levels and in all spheres of the justice system. Occasionally staff support such initiatives; normally, judges do not mind relinquishing managerial tasks, and court clerks may be willing to assume them, especially if they are trained and remunerated for doing so. Visible (and favorable) short-term results are almost a requirement for winning the acquiescence of those who have to assume additional burdens. There will be less resistance to policies that provide more resources; indeed, there may be a tendency to demand excessive budgets.

Reforms That Affect the Demand for Judicial Services

Before attempting to reform the demand side of litigation, one needs information concerning the issues and parties in litigation, the trends in demand, and the prices users pay (attorneys' fees). Even more important are the reasons parties litigate. There is some economic theory that helps to identify the main factors behind

---

[12] This should not go beyond ensuring that people work their assigned hours. An initial quantitative assessment of the Spanish courts found that with the same resources and a minimum of economic rationality, "judicial protection" could be increased 50 to 80 percent.

litigation and the foreseeable changes in response to changing incentives for personnel who work with the legal system. Certain improvements can be made by reducing delays, cutting costs of litigation, amending the regime for allocating procedural costs, or by a number of other measures.[13]

Regarding the demand for judicial protection, it is first advisable to channel through the courts only what is necessary, and to strengthen alternative dispute-resolution mechanisms where they are the superior means of settling the matter. The best-known alternative methods are mediation, arbitration, and conciliation. Others include administrative proceedings, market deregulation, and fact-finding. These alternative mechanisms should be strengthened not only in courts for civil or labor matters, where there is already a tradition of alternative dispute resolution, but also in administrative and criminal courts.[14]

Second, there is no justification for subsidizing all litigation indiscriminately. To discourage excessive and unwarranted demands on the courts, mechanisms such as appropriate court fees can be adopted, or penalties for frivolous litigation.[15] Such reforms to limit demand for judicial protection should weigh both the beneficial effects of deterring excessive litigation and the risk of limiting access to justice. Measures to reduce unnecessary demand result in two sources of savings: they reduce public spending, and save the resources of private parties (monetary or non-monetary) that would otherwise be earmarked for litigation, without substantially affecting the protection of rights. Nonetheless, some professional sectors may resist these measures; in some countries bar associations and other legal professionals have strongly resisted efforts to re-establish or increase the amount of court fees, which might reduce the demand for their services.

Delayed Justice

To illustrate the risks of delay in the justice system, consider a recent phenomenon in Spain: the compulsory release of prisoners held on terrorism and drug-trafficking charges, once the maximum period for pre-trial detention had lapsed. In Costa Rica, to take another example, the backlog in the Constitutional Chamber that hears *amparo* proceedings is considerable. Such delays give rise to possible judicial errors, and also provide vast opportunities for corruption, for those who wish a case to be postponed or decided more quickly.

---

[13] Cooter and Rubinfeld (1989) review the literature on this subject. A simplified presentation of the theory of litigation can also be found in Pastor (1993).

[14] These ADR mechanisms have both good and bad results. See Shavell (1995).

[15] Litigation may also generate external benefits (positive for those who do not bear its costs), so judicial fees should be lower than total costs that stem from lawsuits. But there is quite a gap between such a situation and the subsidy that litigation now enjoys.

As in the areas of judicial reform mentioned thus far, we need information on the scope, characteristics, and evolution of delays. Knowing the distribution of judicial decisions over time and their trends is essential.[16] In addition, this will help us keep references to delays from unjustifiably becoming "the" problem of the whole justice system, and the main subject of the debate.

Assessing why delays occur mainly involves examining what is happening to the supply of and demand for judicial protection, as well as the mechanisms for administering the scarcity, where the system takes in cases based not on price, but on the order in which they arrive. Certain reform policies that can be implemented to cut the delays are mentioned in the previous sections on supply and demand. The point is to increase supply and/or discourage demand, without losing sight of a review of the procedural mechanisms that provide incentives for self-interested or strategic delays.

If the beneficial reduction of delays is justified in terms of costs (i.e., if they are less than the benefits), the result obtained is socially superior. Nonetheless, given that delay is one mechanism for rationing "scarce" judicial services, reducing it may stimulate the demand for judicial protection. Furthermore, social support for policies aimed at reducing delays is the same as that involved in demand for and supply of judicial protection.

Access to Justice

Is there a contradiction between concern over excessive litigation and access to justice? No, because "ni están todos los que son, ni son todos los que están." Neither are all cases there that should be before the courts, nor do all the cases already there merit judicial resolution. The social function of justice, as already noted, is to provide the maximum protection of rights at the least cost, and as far as possible, one should employ other mechanisms that produce similar results.

Equal access to justice requires separating the measures to facilitate access for all citizens, independent of income, from those specifically geared to those who cannot afford to pay.[17] In seeking to ensure access to justice for all, one should review the operation of markets for professional services, a necessary element whose substantial cost is often greater than would be the case were there more competition. In this regard, one must consider the relevance of contingency

---

[16] In legal systems that exercise the most care in this respect, there is information on the matters that are decided upon in each time segment. Most systems have information on cases admitted, resolved, and pending at the end of each year. Even with this poor information, one can prepare indices on the status and trends in the delays. For example, the ratio of cases pending to cases resolved annually suggests the foreseeable workload in years of work.

[17] See Cappelletti and Garth (1978).

fees, advertising, and the organization of a single professional organization for the entire country (if no other solution is possible). Other methods are to prohibit price-setting, examine the conditions of access to the profession, adopt palliative measures to address the asymmetry of information between attorney and client, and eliminate idle interventions by legal professionals (for example, *procuradores*, a special attorney who practices independently and is hired by the client's attorney in order to file matters before the court). In general, freeing up the services markets for these professionals is an important task which, if carried out appropriately, will help ensure greater citizen access to justice.

Concerning access to justice for the poor, it is important to review whether there is sufficient staff, for justice is sometimes one of the most underfunded public programs. In addition, these funds should be better administered, and freedom of choice ensured. The reforms that improve access to justice for all will improve the efficiency with which the service is provided and will reduce the privileges that certain professional groups within the legal community enjoy. Similarly, their resistance will be notable, as already evident in countries where steps have been taken to free the market for legal services.

Some measures to improve access for the poor are more widely accepted than others. Increasing the budgetary resources for public defender rotations (*turnos de oficio*) is generally well regarded by attorneys and *procuradores*. Other measures that increase the competitiveness of markets do not enjoy the same support; it is unlikely that bar associations would support freedom of choice of attorney for the beneficiaries of free justice.

Conclusions

The administration of justice is an essential and inseparable part of the legal system, but it does not receive sufficient attention. An independent, competent, and efficient justice system is required to ensure that rights are made effective, that obligations are performed, and that the rules are observed. Designing a justice system that encourages the creative resources of a society and fosters exchange is a fundamental task that is not sufficiently valued. This task still lies ahead in many countries.

This chapter has reviewed deficiencies common to many judicial sectors, summarized reforms that could ameliorate those shortcomings, and indicated their possible effects, including possible economic impacts. Judicial reform should directly reduce waste and inefficiency and enable the judiciary to better serve its purpose. The effects of such improvement in the efficiency of justice will be felt outside the judicial system as well. To the extent that justice ensures that rights are effectively protected, obligations performed, and rules observed, squandering will be avoided, and incentives will be in place for creating, exchanging information on, and strengthening the various sources of social well-being. Economic development and competitiveness gains are the concrete and specific results of those more general effects.

What budgetary requirements would be posed by a reform such as that considered here? Obviously, it depends on the starting point: the specific reform, and whether it entails creating or adding courts and human or material resources. Nonetheless, in general, judicial reforms do not require enormous budgetary resources.

Moreover, the reforms outlined here would have a high social return with relatively little public expense. In most Latin American countries, if not all, investing in judicial reform is profitable. Where there is a clear shortage of staff, the expenditure entailed is scant and the anticipated return is high. Obviously, this logic applies to those countries where reform does not involve "more of the same," but entails improved management of existing resources.

Those who dare fight for this cause should realize that resistance to change will be formidable. The potential losers are individuals and groups who have stood to gain from inefficiency, bias, and incompetence, some living off idleness and others exploiting the flaws of the judiciary system to their own advantage.

The approach outlined here for reforming the administration of justice may also be useful for tackling problems of justice in very different countries. In any event, applying the social sciences in studying the legal system—especially economics—is essential to ensure proper reform of judicial policy.

References

Cappelletti, M. and Garth, B. (eds.). 1978. *Access to Justice: A World Survey*. Sijthoff and Noordhoff, Lapen aan den Rijn.

Cooter, R. and Rubinfeld, D. 1989. Economic Analysis of Legal Disputes and Their Resolution. *Journal of Economic Literature* (September).

Council of Europe. 1995. *Task Force on Efficiency and Equity of Civil and Criminal Justice*. Strasbourg.

Pastor, S. 1993. *¡Ah de la justicia! Política judicial y economía*. Civitas and Ministry of Justice, Madrid, Spain.

Pedraja, F. and Salinas, J. 1995. La eficiencia de la Justicia. *Revista de Economía Aplicada* 3 (8).

Posner, R. 1985. *The Federal Courts: Crisis and Reform*. Cambridge: Harvard University Press.

Shavell, S. 1995. Alternative Dispute Resolution: An Economic Analysis. *Journal of Legal Studies* 24 (January).

PART II

JUDICIAL
INSTITUTIONS

CHAPTER 8

Governability and
Economic Performance

Alberto Alesina

The 1980s have been called the lost decade for Latin America, a decade when the region saw negative growth rates of per capita GNP. Growth in the region was not spectacular prior to the 1980s either. A striking example is Argentina, which in the early 20th century was among the wealthiest countries in the world. In 1960, Argentina ranked 18th in per capita GNP, ahead of Japan, Greece, and Portugal, and just behind Italy. Today, it's nowhere near that level.

In recent years, economists have sought to explain the wide discrepancies in models of growth across the globe. As economists often do, they first focused on economic variables, such as levels of human capital, measured by the quality and quantity of education, the tendency to save and invest, openness to trade, and the operation of financial markets. The result of this vast literature on the determinants of growth is that even after taking these economic variables into consideration, Latin America as a region has grown *less* in the last three decades than would be expected based on the economic variables alone.

Recent literature tries to explain this observation by reference to political and institutional factors. Here we will consider three of these factors—income distribution, political stability, and bureaucratic efficiency—and how they affect economic growth.

To begin with, income inequality is particularly stark in Latin America as a region. Although major differences exist across countries, Latin America as a region has much worse income distribution than other parts of the world, particularly Southeast Asia. Several authors have pointed to an intense empirical correlation between income inequality and growth. Countries with major disparities in income distribution over the last three decades have simply grown less, even after taking into account other economic explanations of growth. Latin America has grown at a much slower pace than East Asia, for example.

There are several ways to interpret the relationship between income inequality and growth. One explanation has to do with fiscal policy. Major income inequalities lead to demands for redistribution; but efforts to redistribute the income of the wealthy to the poor often lead to unsustainable macroeconomic policies. Such policies, in addition to being unsustainable, are not usually effective in reducing inequality. Populist measures are a typical example: although doing little to correct inequality, they create macroeconomic imbalances, high inflation, and budget deficits. Moreover, redistributive policies that attempt to reduce wide income disparities become a battlefield for different interest groups and rentiers. The resulting redistributive flows rarely improve the social well-being of the poor, while at the same time creating macroeconomic imbalances.

The second explanation concerns the effect of income distribution on political instability and social unrest. It is clear that greater income inequality leads to more political instability, which has negative effects on savings, investment, and growth. Political instability generally has two definitions in academic literature. One is based on the frequency with which governments fall in coups and revolutions; another is based on indices of sociopolitical violence.

In terms of the first definition, Latin America as a region has had military coups in the 1960s, 1970s, and early 1980s with greater frequency than any other region. These conditions bring about the same vicious circle just described: with greater political instability, growth diminishes, yet lower growth is likely to bring even more political instability.

The second way to measure political instability considers the phenomenon of social violence and unrest, based on indices used to compare countries. These indices result from several statistical methods of grouping information culled from many different variables. The variables may include the number of deaths related to political murders; the massive internal violence of civil wars, disturbances, or strikes; and coup attempts. Based on these indicators, numerous countries in Latin America have been very unstable in the last three decades, compared to other countries with a similar level of development. These indices of sociopolitical stability correlate closely with per capita GNP.

The third variable mentioned above, bureaucratic inefficiency and corruption, is of course very difficult to measure. Various indices have been proposed, such as the effectiveness of the legal system and corruption. For example, Paolo Mauro has analyzed the data gathered by Business International, a private organization that establishes national risk indicators, based on questionnaires distributed in various countries.[1] Three indicators seem to be particularly relevant. The first is how the legal environment's *efficiency and integrity* affect business, particularly the business of foreign companies. The second is the *regulatory environment* that foreign companies confront when seeking authorization and permits to operate. The third is *corruption* and the degree to which business transactions entail questionable payments.

See Mauro, Paulo. 1996. *The Effects of Corruption on Growth, Investment and Government Expenditure*. Washington, D.C.: International Monetary Fund.

Data based on these indicators are available for some 70 countries world-wide. Mauro correlated the data with investment and growth, and discovered two things. First, he found that bureaucratic inefficiency and corruption are closely linked to the indicators of political instability, social violence, and income inequality, and all appear to be closely correlated. That an inefficient bureaucracy leads to corruption makes sense, if paperwork requirements have been imposed in order to extract payments for the privilege of bypassing them.

Second, Mauro found that bureaucratic inefficiency and corruption in the judicial system are correlated with low investment and growth. Bureaucratic efficiency, on the other hand, is closely related to political stability and equitable income distribution. There is an initial correlation between growth and income inequality: when high taxes are used to redistribute incomes, they have negative effects on growth.

Nonetheless, other arguments suggest that redistribution may have some positive effects on growth, by reducing political instability and increasing social cohesion. In other words, if redistributive policies could be implemented without compromising macroeconomic equilibrium, perhaps they would not have a detrimental effect on growth.

CHAPTER 9

Protection of Property Rights and Civil Society

Hernando De Soto

The number of the world's developed countries has not changed much since the postwar era, when Japan, Taiwan, and South Korea joined the group. One reason that poorer countries did not advance significantly during the past half century is that they have not yet adopted uniform rules for property. Without rules for property, there can be no market economy, at least not one that lasts. Property rights are fundamental to the legal framework that allows capital markets to function efficiently.

Markets are ancient institutions, of course. Peru had markets for thousands of years, and so did Africa and the Middle East. Indeed, one may recall that Jesus Christ threw the merchants out of the temple because they had turned it into a market. Jesus knew perfectly well what a market was. Evidently there is nothing new about markets; what's new has to do with "property." Property—or rather, the right of ownership in property, as a universal, democratically accessible right—has been widely recognized for less than two centuries. In the case of Japan, for example, it has only been around for 50 years. So this is the major innovation, and this innovation has not reached the third world.

Throughout the third world, registered titles to buildings and real estate in general exist for no more than 50 percent of urban property. In rural areas, only 10 percent of properties have titles. This means, in effect, that 90 percent of the rural properties in Peru, Mexico, Brazil, Indonesia, and Algeria are not titled or registered. From the standpoint of capital investment, this represents total insecurity. It does not mean there are no owners. Owners are decidedly there, and if you try to remove them from the land, you cannot. The domain of such owners is expanding: they have already taken over half of Lima. In 70 to 80 percent of cases, the origin of property rights in Lima is purely informal—property rights without title.

The wave of efforts to create market economies in Latin America will not succeed in the absence of guarantees for property rights. Many forget that since independence from Spain, Latin Americans have attempted structural adjustments and monetary stabilization programs eight times; and after achieving them, we returned to what existed before.

In the 1830s, the first of these crises broke out in the wake of the impossibility of paying debts owed to England, debts for purchases of arms and other materials needed in the struggle for independence. Other crises followed—in 1840, 1870, 1910, 1930, in the late 1970s, the early 1980s, and now in the 1990s. Each time Latin America had debts that we could not pay. The debts were pardoned, interest was capitalized, amortization periods were extended, a macroeconomic adjustment was carried out, the tax system was changed, and trade was liberalized. New loans were provided, the currency was stabilized, the economy was freed up, and railways were transferred to Europeans in payment for new external debts. Then we privatized mines, we privatized industries; and in each case the pendulum swung back five, 10, 15, or 20 years later.

The idea that Latin America has now taken the right path is a bit misguided. This path has been taken eight times. So what was missing? What was missing, to reiterate, is property titles. And we have reason to say so, having witnessed the changes brought about by Peru's government in recent years. Peru has carried out programs on a massive scale to turn informal property into formal property, not only for real properties, but also for enterprises.

The government of Peru has titled and registered approximately 300,000 lots in the Lima area, thereby increasing the value of these assets some 200 percent, apart from market-induced changes in value. In other words, from titling alone, credit has expanded in these areas by 340 percent, and almost 400,000 new enterprises have been incorporated in the formal economy. All these enterprises have seen production increase significantly, along with revenues, and a market economy has begun to operate effectively. Now there is a market for mortgage loans, where there was none before.

On a recent visit to Indonesia, we discussed property rights with some members of the cabinet. Their first question was, how can we establish who owns what, without a registry of where people live throughout the country? Indonesians hold 80 percent of their assets in land, in real property, yet there is no record of who owns what. This poses economic problems: in applying for credit, for example, most of the population cannot use their assets. In addition, it presents security problems, for if guerrilla forces attack, the government cannot control them without having troops throughout the countryside.

So Indonesians already understand the advantages and disadvantages of property rights. For them the essential question is, how do we learn who is the owner of what? I answered them that the information is held by Indonesia's dogs. Travelling through the countryside in Bali, I knew when I was moving from one property to another, because a different dog would bark at me. Their next question was: What enables the Peruvian government to determine who owns a given property? We told them that we identify dogs' barks by means of computers. And in fact, if the dogs only bark up to the edge of their property, then their conduct represents an agreement among members of a society. Clearly, no one will base an investment on dogs' barking, but at least it ensures that no one steals their owner's harvest.

So I explained to the Indonesian legislators how we solved a similar problem. In Peru, ever since the Spanish conquest, there have been 47 attempts to title and register property. Every attempt failed; wherever there are land invasions, the squatters have papers in hand, so there is an inflation of titles. Not only are people occupying lands, but there are also titles, which further complicate things: even in the papers, it is not clear who owns what. In practice, of course, it is known: throughout Peru, it is quite clear who is the owner of every house. Yet one discovers that only by going to the house, as there is no way to find out from a registry.

In Peru we tried to copy what developed countries have done, which is to move from simple to more complex systems of representation. First is the physical universe, consisting of things created in nature or created by man. Then there is a second universe of our minds—the universe by which we visualize things. And there is a third universe, which can be termed universal norms, in which we reach agreement. These norms are a kind of language that enables us to communicate among ourselves about things and about our own relations. If this universe of intentional norms is not complete, then markets cannot function.

The case of property is quite obvious. If I take out a pen, for example, and say this pen is my property, my statement does not establish whether it's your property or mine. Property rights arise from the fact that we both recognize that it is mine. In the abstract, that right exists because we attribute a meaning to ownership of an object, which is the right to exercise control over it. Each intentional norm serves some purpose. For example, mathematics allows us to measure language, speak, write among ourselves; the calendar allows us to organize ourselves in time; money allows us to assign exchange values to things, even to ideas; and property rights allow us to situate things in relation to physical space and in their relationship of control among ourselves. And since property rights do not exist physically, they need to take some embodied form, to which end they must be converted into representations, which we have called institutional instruments. This means that what is abstract is given body so as to confer security on things that are tangible, and that when we use them they give universe one a growing value. They have an almost magical function: once something is in universe one, the physical thing receives a language, a representation in universe three, i.e. in terms of being a universal language. It is then embodied in an instrument and immediately its value begins to rise; that is the secret of language, of property, and of the market economy.

For example, take numbers. If I ask you how much is 349 times 3,278, you will probably have to reach for pencil and paper, use the symbols of mathematics, perform the multiplication, and find a result. In other words, it's not enough to have an answer in memory; you must employ the instruments of mathematics to obtain the result. This is why Einstein said, "My pencil is more intelligent than I." The pencil is an intentional instrument that makes effective use of representations.

The fact that, for example, the zero was added on to numbers made it possible immediately to carry out operations that we otherwise could not imagine. What is interesting to note about property is that dogs bark in all cities of the third world; that is, there is informal recogniztion of property ownership. What's lacking are titles—titles that are duly registered, so as to create legal security.

If titles are issued as they are in Peru by public registries, they are of no value, because no one knows whether they represent anything. In Peru there are, on average, 47 titles per lot, so obviously there is no legal security. The capacity to create valid property titles has yet to be achieved in most of the third world. How can we effectively create those titles? In Peru there was a wide gap between the world of barking dogs and the world of a minority, where some titles had value. Even so, if you applied for a mortgage loan from a Peruvian bank, in most cases they wouldn't grant it.

In essence, our system consisted of building a bridge across the gap. First, we realized that there was not one standard way of obtaining property in Peru, but many ways of occupying or possessing property. There are Andean communities that use literally hundreds of symbols—fences, barriers, gates, and types of agreements—that are not found in the coastal region. In the city, we classified the various forms as *pueblos jóvenes*, private housing cooperatives, state housing cooperatives, and low-income urban development projects (*urbanizaciones populares*). In rural areas, we classified them as indigenous communities, native communities, smallholdings, and beneficiaries of agrarian reform.

After determining the forms of representing property, we began to demonstrate the benefits that property can confer on everyone. Then we undertook the following exercise, which I will outline step by step. The first stage is locating the informal areas and their size. An effort is made to reach consensus on each of the forms that exists for representing property. This is expressed through a social contract that is communicated to the people until they recognize, in effect, that these symbols are theirs. Then institutional reforms are implemented—documenting the institutions of property, identifying obstacles and strategies for removing them, and developing mechanisms to achieve economy of scale. Such mechanisms include assigning responsibility for procedures to a single organization (in Peru, the procedures were divided among 52 state institutions), and then adopting the relevant legislation and regulations.

The second stage is a program for implementation, in which each symbol corresponds to a single national alphabet, which henceforth will be respected. This establishes a single applicable body of law, which nonetheless incorporates all the existing ones. There is a third stage, agricultural surveying and mapping, and a fourth, modernization of the registries, so that with the fifth stage, titling and registration can begin.

This same exercise has been applied with respect to enterprises. There are hundreds of ways to create an enterprise in Peru, and yet the forms can be grouped in nine or ten categories. Those ten categories provide a common denominator, the language of property, that makes it possible to proceed to title and register.

What results has this exercise yielded? In Peru we have succeeded in registering so many properties that property titles are now being used by more than 20 institutions to make loans. By the end of 1996, based on mortgages on these properties, Peruvian institutions were able to extend microcredit or small loans, as most financial institutions do. We have already registered 300,000 titles, and our cost of titling has been $11.30 per lot. Compared to earlier projects financed by the World Bank, the IDB, and U.S. Agency for International Development, which involved two years of research with World Bank consultants, a year with IDB consultants, and another year with consultants from the Universidad Católica of Chile and the University of Arizona, our operation was quite economical. The average price of titling for the international organizations ranged from $5,000 to $17,000 per lot registered, and they titled and registered only about five percent of the number of lots we have registered.

The basic results in Peru's urban sector, from 1990 to 1994, are as follows: the value of the property, independent of changing values in the real estate market, has increased 80 percent to 330 percent, and people have finally begun to pay for electricity and water, making it possible to finance the projects.

Taking measurements in the rural sector was extremely difficult. We decided to measure the number of citrus trees, because it is too difficult to measure tree growth or yield over time. So we compared citrus trees in the areas titled and registered with the contiguous areas that had not been titled and registered. We had experts on citrus trees from California, who reviewed the statistics and determined that it is not water, better location, or better land that makes the difference, but the fact that the land was titled. On average, where we have titled and registered in the first year, output has increased 24 percent to 73 percent. Some 25 percent of the owners who could not obtain credit before are receiving it now. We found that the per capita incomes of farmers with titles and lands clearly divided into lots doubled—from $1,000 to $2,000 annually.

The number of enterprises registered has begun to rise; for now, instead of taking 289 days, it can be done in one day, abiding by the same legal provisions, but fine-tuning them so as to understand the informal language. The result has been the creation of 105,000 enterprises that would not have been established without registration; 276,000 enterprises that were totally informal have joined the formal sector; almost $700,000 has been saved in administrative expenses; $1.27 million has been collected in taxes that would not have been collected; and 500,000 new jobs have been created.

This goes to show that property, like any language when first introduced, has a multiplier effect. Formerly in Peru, when you traveled down a road and saw a house, a lot, or a machine, these properties were idle capital—while in other countries they are living capital, because property rights exist.

In other words, property rights give a thing a second abstract life, which makes is possible not only to use it as a good with a primary function, but as capital, and as a basis for credit. Where the majority of the poor own most of the land, it is not unusual for market economies to fail. How they came to possess the land doesn't matter—in any event, by means more peaceful than those the Spaniards used when they first came to the Americas. But the reality is that their property doesn't have the value it would under capitalism, because they have no title or registration.

As you know, the emerging markets of the future are the markets for infrastructure, meaning for electricity, water, gas, telecommunications, computers and computer applications. It is estimated that private investment expected in those markets between now and the year 2000 to 2005 will pay out some two trillion dollars. These are the largest markets, much larger than the markets of the West, which are growing at 2 percent, compared to our market which, together with those of Asia, the Middle East, and Central Europe, are growing at 15 percent. The issue is not loans from the IDB or the World Bank, but rather those from the international private sector, an amount seven times greater. And now, the international private sector has just discovered the informal sector, and has just found out what happens when effective property titles are not in place.

The international and multinational private sector faces serious obstacles in our countries. Privatization of power companies has begun, but the distribution of power is not complete, and only affects a part of the country. Of every 100 units of electricity generated for distribution in Peru, for example, 34 units are lost due to technical problems, non-technical losses, and failure to pay. In contrast, in the United Kingdom, for every 100 units of electricity that enter the grid, only 6.6 percent is lost. The British power company collects 93.4 percent of the total amount billed, while the Peruvian company collects only 66 percent.

What are the causes of these losses in Lima? When we begin to break them down, we see that these losses do not come from the formal commercial sector, nor from the formal industrial sector, nor from the formal residential sector, but mainly from the informal housing sector, because in effect, the terminals of the infrastructure, whether we're talking about the electric company, the water company, or a telephone company, are houses, and if the house is not titled or registered, you know where the cable or pipe extends to, but you don't know what's behind the pipe and the cable at the terminal point, and if you don't know, there's no way to collect.

This is why privatizing electric power doesn't work. We began with private electricity, and have ended up with public electricity. The private sector can't collect fees where there are no property titles. Even in the formal residential sector there is also an element of informality, which is not due to the lack of title. Instead it is because in the homes of Lima that are registered, in the best sectors of Miraflores, there is a Mrs. Pardo who has 12 clandestine looms in the garage where 14 indigenous people are working making alpaca sweaters for the English market. If that activity is not registered, it's not known who is consuming electricity, and when a substation needs to be installed that has x capacity for distribution, it can blow out within two years due to overload, thereby driving up costs.

In the United Kingdom 6.6 percent of utilities revenue is lost, but in Peru, 34 percent. If we merely cut the informal sector in Lima to half its size, through titling and registration, then one can collect for electricity, as is now being done, and $329 million per year would be brought in in additional revenues.

If that $329 million savings is achieved, we wouldn't need to go back to the IDB, nor to the World Bank, to finance the rest of the country's electrification, because at the present value we have generated enough energy-generating capacity to finance, on our own, the rest of the electric grid. We have studied the different ways electricity is lost, we have seen how electricity is stolen in Peru, and we have a study of more than 110 cases showing how the informal sector taps into the grid. Once the property title is linked to the specific connection, this stealing stops, for the simple reason that the right that defends the property of the poor is no longer political community action, but the same right that defends the private investor who has made an investment, whether in generating, transmitting, or distributing electricity. At the same time, this breaks down the community organization and turns each person into an individual contracting party, who is directly accountable. What is largely perceived abroad as a political risk, the risk of doing business with Peru, is nothing other than the risk that President Fujimori will have to choose between a *pueblo joven*, or shantytown, and a multinational corporation. He will always have to choose the *pueblo joven*, because his power does not come from a multinational, it comes from the votes of that social sector. And as the status of property rights is corrected, these risks diminish, as do interest rates.

What did the developed countries do to get a property rights regime? It's quite simple. The developed countries did the same thing we have done, but in different circumstances. Take the case of Japan. Documents were recently released regarding the U.S. postwar occupation, led by General MacArthur, and half a million dollars have been invested to study that well-known agrarian reform. It is clear that they wanted to effectively democratize property, because MacArthur wanted to decapitate the military feudal order that represented the dangerous militarization of Japan, he wanted to thwart the expansion of communism, which had introduced reforms to property regimes in Russia, and he also wanted to stop the contagion of Mao Tse Tung. After dropping two atomic bombs on Japan, he told them, "you have two years to title and register the entire peasantry," but the documents leave no trace as to how this was done.

Japan had an informal sector strikingly similar to Peru's, based on organizations of impoverished communities called *burakus*, which they legalized, just as we legalized a large part of the institutions of the *pueblos jóvenes* with Fujimori. Some 10,950 collective organizations were titled; they determined who was the owner of what, where the dogs barked. The first step was to take the property register they had inherited during the Meiji restoration, in the late 19th century. That register was forwarded to the ministry of agriculture, which distributed them to the prefectures, which distributed them in turn to the municipalities, and from there they went to the 10,950 *burakus*.

Once that was done, it was possible to determine who was the owner of what, because these families had been the owners of these properties for 400 years. It so happened that the feudal lord had the property on paper, but actually the worker had property over the land, but not the right to convey it to the market economy.

Then the Japanese citizens were given an explanation as to what had happened. First, the false representation of property was brought to an end, and that was the end of the public registry, equivalent to what we have in Peru. The information was obtained directly from the citizens affected, the new registry was created, and little by little the titling process began.

Take another example: In the early 20th century Switzerland was the poorest country in Europe. It was so poor that an old article in the Swiss Constitution provides for state control over travel agencies, to ensure that they would not be used as a means for *exporting* cheap labor. Another article of the Swiss Constitution prohibits Swiss citizens from being recruited to work in foreign armies.

A group of university students undertook to study the different ways property was actually distributed in Switzerland. They were able to consolidate it into a single language, a single currency, and this currency was brought before the federal council. In the next seven years it was forward to the parliament, and Switzerland began to have a single regime of property rights, and a form of title that became hard currency. Today no one questions the fact that Switzerland has the most secure property system in the world, and it is one of the wealthiest countries in Europe, after having been the poorest country in all of Europe 80 years ago.

The same thing happened in Germany. There, everyone knew who was really the owner, but in 1806 Napoleon had to win a tremendous battle against the Germans at a time when the Germans could not recruit troops, for them to realize titling and registering property would enable them to do so; in 1807 a reform began that lasted until Bismarck's day. They consolidated the form property rights would take, and the land tenure system, in order to raise an army, but in so doing created a market economy. Of course, Germany's history shows how they defeated the French and created the German Republic; and it should be recalled that they also created property rights and one of the most prosperous countries in Europe.

The United States expanded based on land invasions that created shanty-towns and other informal forms of property, from the time of the California Gold Rush until the taking of lands in Florida, with no agricultural surveys or geometric calculations of the land, which was later legalized. They were able to consolidate the legal status of all property in the late 19th century. Property rights in the United States came up from below, and were then incorporated into the legal system.

In conclusion, the question is: What are the major obstacles today to giving the third world property rights? Essentially, this task involves legal action, which is necessary for the market economy to operate. For example, it used to be that in Peru 102 bureaucratic procedures were required to title and register a property, which all told took 1,896 days. Now, if you are a poor Peruvian, we have reduced it to 120 days. Of all the reductions made of superfluous and useless issues, half were technical, the other half legal. Diminishing the legal steps required breaking down the monopoly that had been held by the public notaries of Lima, who numbered only 40, and succeeding in an effort to have 90,000 lawyers authorized to carry out the same functions as notaries. In order to title a property, it had been necessary to review and certify a document 29 times; now, the same document must be reviewed and certified only three times. The same holds for engineers: a blueprint in a *pueblo joven* in Peru required the signature of not one, but 19 engineers—so that if the house collapsed in an earthquake, you didn't know which of the 19 was accountable. Reducing this to one engineer cut the time and made the process much simpler.

Yet while there is a historic record that we can draw on, because we have done nothing the Japanese, Swiss, or English hadn't done, there is now an additional obstacle that did not exist before, the world of property rights. Some 90 percent of the money supposedly spent to generate property rights in our countries is not invested in lawyers or jurists, but in engineers, who have cornered the market. In other words, in any property-related project in Latin America, those who win out in competitive bidding (ultimately financed by funds from the multilateral institutions) are engineers, people involved in mapping, people who do agricultural surveys and who sell equipment. This makes sense in the developed countries, where they achieve millimetric precision, but it is perfectly useless in our case.

Consequently, for example, in a project in the Northeast of Brazil, involving a $30 million loan, $25 million was used to map that part of the Northeast. Yet to date, according to reports from the Brazilians, no registered title has yet to be distributed to a single peasant. They have beautiful maps of all Brazil, just as we have beautiful maps of all Peru, but the maps don't represent property rights, property rights are the legal side. We must overcome our long-standing misconceptions about property and legal security.

We now face an additional enemy, technology. There should be a moratorium on additional expenditures for new machinery that does not define property rights, but merely records physical measurements. This is like giving someone a typewriter without first teaching him the alphabet. Once the physical space is defined, one can store the information in a computer, with a map, to determine precisely where the property is in relation to the North Pole, with an error of only five centimeters; but today in Lima we don't need to know how many centimeters we are from the North Pole. What we need to know is how many centimeters one must be from the Rímac river; and all that can be done without importing a single piece of machinery from abroad, using just what we have in Peru.

Based on these arguments, it is clear that law is not insulated from the rest of society; rather, the law affects economic development. And the revolution of the economy and the market will not occur if that law does not come to prevail. The rest is just a question of putting together larger budgets to reform the judicial systems. The law must be reformed to make way for the market economy, so as to be able to guarantee the rights of those citizens who are poor.

CHAPTER 10

Judicial Reform
and Civil Society

Luis Pásara

Judicial reform is now so central to the public agenda that it hardly matters who is putting forth the agenda. Many groups that advocate new government policies give judicial reform a high priority. Behind this apparent consensus, however, are different and conflicting points of view regarding the problems of the judicial sector.

Demands on the Justice System

First, citizens are notoriously dissatisfied with the justice system, as many opinion polls reflect. Latin Americans usually view the administration of justice as slow, tending to favor those in power, and corrupt, although in varied degrees from one country to the next. In the case of Central America, there is widespread discontent with respect to the political nature of judicial appointments, and interference and pressure brought to bear on judges' decisions.[1] All these characteristics converge in the functioning of the judicial apparatus, which, as our literature suggested long ago, provokes distrust among the citizenry in most of the region.

A second source of discontent is linked to the functioning of the economy. A Peruvian study emphasizes that "...poor administration of justice implies that one cannot demand the performance of contractual terms," which leads to "greater risk." (Ortiz de Zevallos 1994) It is precisely this greater risk that led the World Bank to include judicial reform among the conditionalities on its loans. To contribute to this effort, the World Bank and the Inter-American Development Bank are financing studies and programs to overhaul the judiciaries in several countries of the region.

The concern with justice on the part of these international organizations is closely related to structural reform programs they have supported in Latin Amer-

---

[1] As reported in surveys taken by Florida International University's Center for the Administration of Justice.

ica. Through programs to modernize the state, promoted and co-sponsored by multilateral institutions, administrative authorities have seen their regulatory capability diminish considerably. This fact, together with promotion of the private sector as a leading player, and competition as the driving force of the system, gives the judiciary a more central role in solving economic disputes. And although having recourse to such courts on a regular basis has not become a key concern for businesspersons of the region, it is such a concern for international capital. Foreign firms are less skillful at dealing with local power structures, and they perceive a need for an institutional framework to minimize the risks associated with their move into the region.

Third, we are facing a political demand. For large contingents of the electorate, the return to democracy cannot be limited to periodic consultations at the polls. Many of our citizenry are disillusioned with politics, after seeing power abused by both the executive and legislative branches. This disillusion is greater than when the problem seemed to originate in successive military governments, which were not subject to legal control. Certainly recent experiences in Latin America, with two presidents removed from their posts, suggest the importance of institutional mechanisms that can check the exercise of power.

Once again, the judiciary is called on to fulfill this role, which citizens perceive as part of democratic government. It is proposed that the judiciary effectively exercise its oversight role with respect to other branches of government in the manner usually prescribed in our constitutions, but which in fact is only occasionally put into practice by the judges. If the judiciary assumes this responsibility, which it can and should do, it could help make the courts in our countries "a guarantee of legitimacy." (Peña 1992a)

Another reason for discontent with our judicial systems stems from the increasingly central place of human rights in our countries. During the worst times in Latin America's difficult experience of recent decades, human rights have been a dead letter in our constitutions and laws; even now this continues to some extent. The merely declaratory nature of norms that were regularly ignored by repressive practices—police and even judicial practices—is a responsibility of judges who lacked the knowledge, zeal, or courage to defend the human rights proclaimed by law.

Finally, there is an internal demand to make changes to the judicial system. Several organizing initiatives timidly reveal some discontent among those who work in and with the judiciary. It is true that demands from within the judiciary usually take little stock of citizens' interests in the matter. But a "bad conscience" with respect to judicial practice is beginning to extend to more than a few countries.

In summary, this is not just an ambiguous demand to modernize judicial institutions where files are still hand-sewn, in an age when they should be using computers. The urgent needs we face have been spelled out by Javier de Belaúnde for the Peruvian case: "There is a growing sense of juridical insecurity, of lack of protection of citizens in the face of violence and abuse ... structural impunity for those who violate the law ... an ever louder call for respect for the fundamental rights and public freedoms ... and justice has remained bound to the structure of colonial society." (Belaúnde 1994)

The administration of justice is in serious crisis not only because of unmet demands, but also due to what Peña (1992a) has called "the trained incapacity" of the judges to respond to them. In this sense, as the Grupo de Estudios Constitucionales observed in Chile, the crisis of justice reflects not so much the inability to meet demand, but institutional ineptitude when it comes to taking note of defects, assessing problems, designing improvements, and responding to the challenges posed by society.

Alternative Mechanisms and Their Risks

Alternatives to the judicial sector have arisen to deal with disputes that the justice system does not resolve adequately. Three alternative mechanisms can illustrate this, as follows:

• Arbitration to settle disputes between companies or business groups. For economic interests of a certain magnitude, this is an effective and efficient way to resolve conflicts, based on explicit criteria, in a relatively brief time frame, and at reasonable cost.

• Use of the communications media for proceedings parallel to those undertaken, or that should be undertaken, by the justice system of the state. They include accusations, investigations, and social sanctions, especially for those who might receive benign or lenient treatment by judges. In this regard, the communications media in our countries are deemed much more trustworthy than the courts.

• Social "activism" whereby people take justice into their own hands, by *justicieros* or gunmen who use force to defend what they consider theirs. Private justice by groups may range from the trials held by peasant organizations and the community lynchings in Peru and Guatemala, to the death squads that assassinate "undesirables" in Brazil and Colombia.

These three substitutes for the judicial system are responses to the lack of action from the state's justice system. This failure of justice gives rise first to frustrated social expectations, and then to the rise of escape valves that seek to achieve results more efficiently, and under necessary and well-defined societal checks and balances.

These mechanisms, which do not involve courts, are welcomed by those who promote the increased use of alternative dispute resolution. As long as the state does not relinquish its essential functions, other mechanisms and forums for settling certain disputes can undoubtedly be effective. But which matters for litigation can we remove from the state judiciary without weakening its basic role in society? The answer is not technical, but political, and should be adopted, by consensus, by each society. Certain risks implicit in the possible options should be noted, however.

Behind the extreme proposals to make ADR more widespread (some of which even speak of "restoring" the function of administering justice to society), lurk several serious dangers:

• In social contexts marked by major inequalities, alternative dispute resolution mechanisms have yet to solve problems of inequality between parties and blatant interference by the constituted authorities. These problems have always beset the state justice system, which attempted to address them with notoriously poor results. Nothing guarantees that the alternative mechanisms will be more successful.

• In highly differentiated societies, the "return" may produce a justice system that serves a plurality, or a particular class or social stratum—"to each his own justice"—whose very different qualities would take us back to something like the *fueros personales*. In a system where jurisdiction of a court over a defendant is based on domicile, the already existing differences among strata and quality of life are reproduced in the realm of dispute resolution. In Peru's case, often cited as a paradigm of non-state peasant justice, the *rondas* administer justice with little regard to the guarantees of due process, and in some cases little respect for human rights (Zarzar 1991).

• Excessive societal decentralization of the task of administering justice, and the consequent construction of very different private paradigms for solving social conflicts, may precipitate the dissolution of public and community life, already found in some national situations with fragmented societies or incomplete processes of nation-building.

Should current conditions remain unchanged, the use of alternative dispute resolution will certainly increase. Many may still prefer the old judicial apparatus, since "the uncertainty generated by poor functioning leads those who are non-compliant or who act in bad faith to find an appropriate forum for eluding their responsibilities." (Ortiz de Zevallos 1994)

Unburdening the judiciary of the weight of a certain number of cases for resolution elsewhere will relieve, but not resolve, its complex set of problems, nor does it circumvent the need for the judiciary to operate efficiently. Moreover, this would leave unresolved the political demand that has been raised, which even the best forms of judicial privatization cannot satisfy. Effective checks on the political branches of government will require a much more independent judiciary than can be found in most of the region today.

Judges Who Fail to Respond to Demands

We will now focus on the role of judges and courts, mindful that the justice system encompasses many more elements. The greatest obstacle to trial judges embracing the conduct sought by some social demands is the strict adherence to legal form and the letter of the law that is reflected in the actions of most of our judicial officers. This strict adherence does not stem from an inevitable legal obligation, as some spokespersons of the judiciary explain by way of excuse. It is part of the prevailing legal culture, which is very strong in shaping practices.

Peña (1992b) argues, based on the Chilean experience, that the problem is that the judges "appear to be more committed to the means than to the ends of the legal system." Along the same lines, Zaffaroni (1994) has written that the Argentine judiciary is characterized by "ritualistic attitudes or conduct that entail abiding by all formal requirements in a reiterative, obsessive, and submissive fashion, forgetting or relegating the substance and objectives of the function." Zaffaroni adds that "appealing to any formal recourse" is also useful for judicial officers to avoid "any decision that may give rise to conflicts."

For Dromi (1992), the prevailing trend among Argentine judges is a "bureaucratic culture" that only takes account of "everything that's in the case file, [and] nothing that isn't." Herrendorf (1994) agrees with Dromi, and describes the Latin American judge as "a bureaucratic official, crushed by case files, poorly paid, more interested in getting rid of the pending cases than producing revolutionary case law by handing down historic judgments."

In Peru, one judge has identified strict adherence to the letter of the law as a typical component of the bureaucratic attitude: "Judicial decisions are limited to reproducing the text of the law." (Sánchez Palacios 1994) But Barros (1991) has observed, studying the Chilean case, that recurring to the law in formalistic fashion may hide a more serious problem:

> There is decadence in the reasoning of the judgments, and insecurity as to the criteria for decision-making is mounting. The cause, contrary to what one commonly hears, must be sought more in judicial subjectivism than in formalism. Legal formalism is more an excuse that distracts attention from the issue of judicial responsibility. The reticent attitude of the courts in the area of fundamental rights, for example, has been justified by the argument that the judges' only job is to apply the law. Nonetheless, it can be shown that the problem does not stem from a rigid and inexorable professional

technique of our higher-ranking judges. Suffice it to contrast the very strict criteria for interpretation adopted in cases of abuse of public authority, with the light manner with which clearly discretional criteria are embraced when ruling on complaint appeals (*recursos de queja*).

Ritual adherence to form, bureaucratic practices that favor means over ends, the literal interpretation of a statute in the guise of law (and opportunistic departures from it), are some of the defects identified by those who analyze judicial practices in Latin America. Indeed, the greatest obstacle to accepting change is to be found in those aspects of the judicial mindset. As Zaffaroni observes (1994), one finds in that judicial culture not so much "an authentic choice for a conservative ideology," but "a trained resistance to change" of the sort found in institutions "organized on the authoritarian model."

An analysis of judicial decisions reveals that this culture of the judge is reflected in work output through the following:

- Insufficient weight accorded the Constitution. A legalist bias in the professional training of judges, which is focused on the codes--with special attention to the procedural codes--silently interprets the Constitution as containing norms eminently declaratory in nature that cannot be enforced, unless channelled through the regular legal rules. Until this happens, the Constitution does not exist in the daily practice of many Latin American judges.

- Refusal to interpret the law, opting instead for a literalist approach. Many judges think that the law does not need to be interpreted, as it has only one possible meaning. By considering themselves as mere enforcers, judges renounce ab initio any responsibility to introduce innovations and creativity into the law in deciding cases.

- Passivity in the process. Ritualistic formalism, bureaucratic behavior, and lack of legal interpretation all contribute to this posture of judges in the judicial process, both civil and criminal. In effect, they renounce the legal possibilities of giving the law direction, leaving it instead to those who are able to take initiative. One well-known example is the case of persons held in pretrial detention who have no attorney: they will remain in detention, and may never even get a verdict. Someone else has to "move the case," for the judge will not.

- Distance from reality. When one recurs in excess to the formalities of the law, for example, in weighing evidence, it becomes impossible to reconcile the facts of the case with the version that comes out in the courts. By using such devices, our judges reproduce a sort of professional schizophrenia: on the one hand, they embrace a legal discourse in which, for example, penalties are aimed at social redemption of the criminal; on the other hand, one finds a scandalous social reality that shouts the opposite message outside the courtroom.

- Failure to consider the social and economic effects of judicial decisions. If the judge merely applies the legislator's dictates, whatever happens as a result of the application of the law is not the judge's responsibility. This argument is often used by the judicial authorities to respond, in their own manner, to the social criticisms leveled at the justice system, which they really don't understand. Most Latin American judges lack the criteria to take up such criticisms, which place responsibility on them, and not just on the law, for the poor outcomes reflected in the administration of justice.

Based on the foregoing, it can be argued that a significant proportion of those currently employed as judicial officers in Latin America are not qualified to assume the roles expected of a judge. Limited professional training in many cases qualifies them only for weak legal reasoning. Without understanding the legal order as an organic whole, under the Constitution, they tend to operate through the isolated use of disjointed legal rules, preferably procedural ones. Consequently, their weak professional training seeks shelter in a legalistic and formalistic culture, resisting the challenge of innovation and creativity, through case law, that is increasingly demanded by the public.

Reforms Being Attempted

On the one hand, in Latin America many demands are being made on justice systems. On the other hand, those systems suffer from a "trained incapacity," clothed in legalism, formalism, and ritualism, to respond to such demands. The result is the present crisis, as well as a number of reform initiatives.

The political authorities have taken charge of the issue, with different degrees of seriousness. For example in Peru, the 1992 *autogolpe* followed an effort to appoint judges by an alternative mechanism that enjoyed a certain degree of consensus. In Chile, President Eduardo Frei dedicated much of his May 1994 speech before the legislature to explaining why his government will promote in-depth reforms to the administration of justice. In Mexico, President Ernesto Zedillo inaugurated his term in December 1994, by announcing that judicial reform would be a key objective of his government, which immediately thereafter became absorbed in an economic emergency.

International agencies are also placing priority on judicial reform. The United Nations Development Programme, the World Bank, the Inter-American Development Bank, and the Inter-American Institute of Human Rights are all engaged in long-term activities aimed at transforming Latin America's justice systems. These organizations, among others, have joined the United States Agency for International Development (AID), which since the 1980s has earmarked significant sums to support a series of institutional improvements in the justice systems, mainly in Central America. In only five years, AID invested almost $7 million to strengthen judicial systems (USAID 1993).

This general picture confirms that the issue is receiving considerable attention. Nonetheless, when one looks more closely, it appears that in several countries, parallel reform efforts are under way that fail to take cognizance of one another. In Central America, thanks to resources provided by both the United States and Europe, judges and prosecutors go through dozens of training courses annually designed by working groups set up in one or another public institution, with various sources of financing. These efforts are sometimes based on rather elementary assessments that do not take account of the shortcomings and needs of the respective judiciaries, nor do they know what has been done by others who came before them. Proposals for activities are often designed that fail to address the specific problems of the country in question. And one can easily verify the existence of standard proposals that are promoted by some organizations in all the countries. The clearest example involves the judicial schools, which are invariably prescribed throughout the region. These courses, often offered in a routinely bureaucratic fashion, cover a wide variety of subjects without any sense of priorities and without motivating the participants. Some include additional elements that distract judicial officers from their essential tasks.

In evaluating the various efforts under way, the key question is whether the main issues facing the judiciary are being addressed. Unfortunately, these reform efforts are carried out despite a lack of reliable data, and with insufficient analysis of the root causes of judicial problems. The failure of such programs to understand how justice really works in our countries leads to certain predictable results, as follows:

• Excessive attention to the aspects of institutional design, as if the conduct of the actors in the judicial system were actually totally dependent on the structure and rules adopted by the institutions.
• Concentration of reform activities in areas such as training and management, which are certainly not useful for solving structural problems such as those which plague the appointments system, and the use of computers, whose incorporation into the courts cannot solve the problems posed by the attitude of the personnel who work in the judiciary.

Strategy and Key Players

What's missing in programs for judicial reform now under way in the region, we submit, are appropriate strategies, objectives and means. Strategies are needed to coordinate the various parties interested and involved in the subject, and determine what functions can and should be performed by the administration of justice. Step-by-step objectives must be based on strategic priorities. Finally, appropriate means should be found to achieve these objectives. This means reaching agreement as to who the players are and how they should focus their efforts to transform the justice systems.

How can such a strategy be defined? And who should make it possible? To date, various efforts to reform the administration of justice in our countries came from one of two channels: intervention from outside the judiciary, generally from the executive or the legislature, that reorganized, removed, and/or imposed certain reforms; or a charge entrusted to the judiciary itself to design and adopt the reforms it deems advisable. In the Peruvian case, where both channels have been used in turn, neither produced exemplary results.

Intervention from outside the judiciary has led to legal changes that were later sabotaged or assimilated into old attitudes and practices. In open defiance or through powerful forces of inertia, this kept in place the state of affairs that was supposed to be changed. Resistance from judges, which ensued in several cases as a result of institutional changes imposed without decisions by the actors affected, has reinforced the judicial fallacy according to which experience is the equivalent of knowledge. Worse still, it has given rise to a "vaccine effect"—the judicial reform is now seen by some as an outside attack, the result of the failure to understand the issues facing the judiciary, which can only truly be understood by the judges. In summary, outside imposition seems to make it all the more difficult to bring about changes in the mindset of judges capable of reshaping institutionalized judicial practices.

The second, induced in many countries by proposals from international cooperation agencies, has not produced significant improvements either. In several cases, under political pressure, the top-level judicial authorities have accepted embarking on a process that has become bogged down in bureaucratic traps, such as commissions that never conclude their work or whose conclusions are filed indefinitely, or that have limited their objectives to secondary aspects of judicial operations, with results of practically no significance for the system as a whole. An in-depth evaluation of judicial reform in Honduras casts light on this process, in both lines of work (AID 1993).

Repeated efforts at judicial reform from within seem to indicate that judicial bodies are incapable of reforming themselves. For if those who determine the contents, level, and timing of the changes are mainly those at the head of the judiciary, their resistance to change is likely to be greater than their convictions about the need for reform. The reason is obvious: any change alters a state of affairs whose beneficiaries include those at the top of a highly hierarchical pyramid.

However, judges must participate in the tasks of the reform. The cases of

Spain and Italy suggest that in a process of transformation of the justice system, those who seek and support this process "from within" play a crucial role. In such cases, these players were not members of the upper echelons of the judiciary, but judges from different courts and places who came together freely and organized, democratically, to deal with their dissatisfaction and their quest for change outside of the hierarchically structured bodies of the judiciary. And such judges are to be found in many of our countries.

But not only judges should participate actively in advancing the reform. If judicial reform is to be viable, it must go beyond the judicial sphere and find a place on the public agenda. Although judicial reform should not be primarily a politicized issue, it is inevitably political. It is therefore necessary for society as a whole to participate in reforming the administration of justice, in varying degrees and different ways.

The Role of Civil Society

The demand that civil society should be part of the transformation of the justice system appears to be corroborated by failed efforts at judicial reform. The activities of judicial institutions and the efforts to transform them do not unfold in a vacuum, but are highly conditioned by their relationship to society as a whole. Thus judicial reform is never an "internal" matter, but is inevitably social and political, because configurations of power will be altered if the reform is successful, or consolidated should it fail.

Of the various social actors involved, politicians constitute a key sector. The members of a country's political elite, the decision-makers, must be convinced of the importance of a reform that truly institutionalizes the judiciary as a socially reliable place for settling disputes and for placing checks on power. Institutionalizing the social, economic, and political conflicts means that the elite will not directly control the solutions applicable to each of them. But it also means that a much more stable regime will be in place, in both political and economic terms, making it possible to plan all of the country's activities on a permanent basis, not subject to the outcome of the next elections. Clearly the political elite stands to gain much more in the long run than it might lose in the way of diminished power, by establishing an independent judiciary whose effective action confers legitimacy on the system and improves the country's standing. The judicial reformers will have to make a major effort to persuade the governing elite as to the advisability of the reform.

While politicians play a crucial role in giving impetus to the judicial reform process, political parties should not be the only social actors involved. All of the social sectors are called on to participate, because the matter pertains to all of them. To call for the active incorporation of other sectors to the judicial reform process in countries with a highly dense social fabric will be simple; in other countries, in contrast, it will require a wide-ranging educational initiative aimed at having citizens "discover" the issue as an important matter on the public agenda.

Citizens are generally absent from discussions on justice. Citizens are discontent with the justice system, but are not involved in justice reform. The common citizen, passive and disorganized with respect to the justice system, merely suffers its effects. When coming before the courts out of the need to have a right recognized, or subpoenaed to defend himself from an accusation, a citizen must put up with the ills of the system—its costs, its slow pace, and its criteria for decision-making—with a certain degree of impotence. In other words, the citizen is at the mercy of whatever the administration of justice offers, unable to exercise any influence in amending its structure.

In contrast to other areas of state management, the justice system does not appear on the political agenda; justice system reform is not to be found in the programs or platforms of those who seek to garner the backing of the electorate. The electorate, concerned about many issues it hopes are taken up by the political representatives, does not include justice among the social priorities. The existing discontent does not translate into a political demand.

This constraint stems from both the sacralization and incomprehensibility with which the administration of justice has cloaked itself, as a preventive measure, and in its treatment of all matters in isolation from one another. A particular case is rarely seen as a specific instance of a more general problem that can be identified with a given social sector. Only cases involving scandals arouse such interest on the part of the public (but not in all the countries). In such circumstances the consideration of the case by the courts appears to be especially careful, and usually produces a result different from that originally anticipated. But the average case, in which a citizen suffers the conditions of the justice system, does not spark any mobilization or make its way into the news. The horrors of those average cases stir up indignation only in those who suffer them, in isolation from one another, but they do not amount to a social demand for radical judicial reform. This lack of such demand is key in maintaining the current state of affairs, and thus must be addressed by any reform program that seeks to be effective.

Two examples illustrate this point in different ways. In Honduras, the judicial reform sponsored by AID (1993) included an item for citizen education, which was to produce mass knowledge of citizen rights and duties vis-à-vis the justice system. The judicial apparatus of Honduras succeeded in having the respective programmed deferred—forever, it turns out, as it was never carried out—with the argument that better citizen education would lead to greater demands on a judiciary not yet able to respond to them. The blockage of this program displays the undeniable cunning of those who didn't really want the reform to proceed.

The other example is a positive one. In Argentina, until the 1994 constitutional reform, higher-level judges were appointed by the president of the republic, with the consent of the Senate. In 1993, the appointments process began, in response to the need for new criminal courts for oral and public trials then being introduced. The civic group *Poder Ciudadano* called on the citizenry to send background information on proposed candidates to the Senate Confirmation Committee members, whose names and phone numbers were announced on television. As a result of many allegations and disclosures, the government had to withdraw some of the names initially submitted. For the first time, the general public had been able to participate, albeit informally, in the judicial appointments process.

The first example shows that those who oppose changes know very well that reforms may be furthered by active citizen participation. The second case shows that it can happen.

Only the participation of civil society will guarantee that a certain degree of social control over the system appears not only at the end of the reform process, as a result of it, but that it will also guide, lead, and amend it, to guarantee that it is carried out. Without such citizen participation, justice, like any bureaucracy, will tend to turn inward. This attitude has brought our justice systems to crisis, and it must not be allowed to take root again.

As for the notion of civil society, all of us citizens are part of civil society insofar as we are able to associate with one another to aggregate interests and obtain a certain level of representation. While this is clear, one of those trends now in vogue, which Latin Americans are inclined to follow, tacitly makes the non-governmental organizations (NGOs) subjects of civil society. NGOs are often important promoters and catalysts of civil society but, in the absence of a strong social fabric, fall into the temptation to replace civil society. So when it is proposed that civil society play an active role in judicial reform, it is not just a question of bringing the directors of a few NGOs to sit down at the table. Instead, citizens—all or many citizens—must participate in the reform process, make it their own, and induce their political and social representatives to seek the appropriate solutions.

This also requires a process of citizen education. In reaction to the ineffectiveness of the judicial system and exacerbated by skyrocketing crime, an authoritarian and primitive vision of justice has come to prevail in our countries. This heavy-handed approach to criminals—including a certain cry for the death penalty, which has no deterrent force—reflects the worst kind of retributive justice. In such a view, the principle of "innocent until proven guilty" hardly appears to exist, and this is also true for many basic human rights.

Based on that same view, the "judicial purges" that several governments have applied to corrupt or maverick judicial bodies have been viewed favorably, as beneficial measures, the necessary sanction for an errant system. These measures often produce negative results, however. Instead, we must aim for an *independent* judiciary—not subject to the dictates of whoever is in power—which can be entrusted with the task of settling disputes. Massive citizen education on justice and human rights is needed for this to come about.

The task appears enormous, and it is. Nonetheless, in Latin America these are auspicious times to build a different kind of administration of justice. Several factors are now favorable to help attain this objective. We should take advantage of the opportunity available for uprooting one of the oldest and costliest ills to plague our countries.

References

Barros, E. 1991. Notas sobre la naturaleza de la función judicial. In *Cuadernos de análisis jurídico*. No. 18. Santiago, Chile: School of Law, Universidad Diego Portales.

Belaúnde, J. de. 1994. Institucionalidad jurisdiccional del Poder Judicial. In *Nuevas perspectivas para la reforma integral de la administración de justicia en el Perú*. Lima: Ministry of Justice.

Dromi, R. 1992. *Los jueces. ¿Es la justicia un tercio del poder?* Buenos Aires: Ed. Ciudad Argentina.

Herrendorf, D. 1994. *El poder de los jueces. Cómo piensan los jueces que piensan.* Buenos Aires: Abeledo-Perrot.

Ortiz de Zevallos, G. 1994. Costos y acceso a la administración de justicia. In *Nuevas perspectivas para la reforma integral de la administración de justicia en el Perú*. Lima: Ministry of Justice.

Peña, C. 1992a. Poder judicial y sistema político. Las políticas de modernización. In *Cuadernos de análisis jurídico*. 22. Santiago, Chile: School of Law, Universidad Diego Portales.

_____. 1992b. ¿A qué nos obliga la democracia? Notas para el debate sobre la reforma judicial. In *Cuadernos de análisis jurídico*. No. 22. Santiago, Chile: School of Law, Universidad Diego Portales.

Sánchez Palacios, M. 1994. Formación y capacitación de magistrados. In *Nuevas perspectivas para la reforma integral de la administración de justicia en el Perú*. Lima: Ministry of Justice.

USAID. 1993. *A Strategic Assessment of Legal Systems Development in Honduras.* Technical Report No. 10. Arlington: United States Agency for International Development.

Zaffaroni, E. 1994. *Estructuras judiciales.* Buenos Aires: Ed. Ediar.

Zarzar, A. 1991. Las rondas campesinas de Cajamarca: de la autodefensa ¿al autogobierno? In Luis Pásara et al., *La otra cara de la luna. Nuevos actores en el Perú*. Buenos Aires: Ed. Manantial.

CHAPTER 11

Modernization, Democratization and Judicial Systems

Jorge Correa Sutil

The justice system has become a focus of public debate and reform efforts in Latin America as never before. Proposed reforms extend well beyond the allocation and use of resources, to constitutional and procedural matters as well. The public agenda is replete with plans to create judicial councils, increase the number of courts, establish training programs, make courts more specialized, promote alternative dispute resolution, expand access to justice, streamline procedures, and strengthen public defender offices. Indeed, there are far more proposals for change than judicial systems are able to absorb.

Increasing Relevance of Judicial Systems

Throughout the world, judicial systems are gaining importance in day-to-day life in a way that has no comparison with the situation of fifty or even ten years ago. In Italy, judges combating corruption have literally changed history, and will surely be seen as the principal actors initiating a period of political and social harmony. Italian children today probably know more names of judges than of cabinet members. Spain is undergoing similar reforms, to the point that any politician knows the best candidate to put up in an election is a judge who has played a prominent role in fighting corruption.

Turning to Latin America, the process is not very different. In most countries of the region, judges have before them the central, most controversial problems facing society. For example, Colombia gives enormous responsibility to its judges in the struggle against drug trafficking and violence, which are now the country's most pressing issues. In Mexico, the capacity of the judicial system to prosecute political crimes will be crucial for future stability. In Peru, the power of the judiciary was President Fujimori's main argument to justify his break with the constitutional process that brought him to office. In Venezuela, the military movements in February 1994 that came close to destabilizing the political regime relied in part on the accusation that the judicial system was not capable of investigating and judging cases involving political corruption.

In Chile and Argentina, as elsewhere, the transition to democracy has called for the judicial resolution of past human rights violations. And the democratization process in Uruguay is inseparable from transforming legal procedures and strengthening the judiciary.

Modern economies cannot develop without efficient systems for conflict resolution, and the stability of democracies depends heavily on the judicial system. In all our countries, the most pressing problems end up on the judges' desk. Defending the environment, combating organized crime, issues of sexual morality, adequate circulation of credit, the cost of economic transactions, protection of property rights, protecting minorities, ensuring open political processes, and all other issues of public significance, end up in the hands of judges for final resolution.

Comparing these circumstances with those of 15 or 20 years ago, when judiciaries were relatively immune to ideological influences and political events in our countries during the 1970s, we see now a judiciary in the midst of transformation, at the center of our history, and under the attentive gaze of the citizenry. It is not surprising, then, that international agencies are displaying unprecedented interest in improving these judicial systems. The judicial systems are a key element in our countries' efforts to achieve their objectives of political democratization, modernization, and opening of the economic and social welfare systems. Perhaps this growing importance of judicial systems is, therefore, the first sign to recognize in the process of transformation now under way that we call "modernization."

Directions of Change

In sum, judicial systems are either undergoing change, or are the subject of proposals for change, at the same time they have become more visible and more important in the public affairs of the region. Exploring the causes of both phenomena will help us to identify the forces behind such changes, and to better understand them.

The process of change in the judicial sector is clearly linked to other changes in society and in the state structures—a process often termed modernization. These transformations are leading to a series of new demands on the judiciary, exposing its incapacity to respond adequately to them. Recognizing these trends and these demands is the first step toward evaluating the relative importance, urgency, and pertinence of the proposals that abound in public debate today.

Modernization and Democratization

Across the political spectrum in Latin America, democratization and modernization have become guideposts for the economic and political changes under way. The region's judicial systems will need to "keep up with the times" and respond to the tasks set by development. What follows are some aspects of these changes that will set challenges for the judicial agenda.

Economic Liberalization and Internationalization

Opening the economy results in diversification of the means of commerce in goods and services. Liberalization entails new forms of circulation of credit and money (including electronic), and of goods and services. Forms of contracts also change— both principal and ancillary agreements (insurance and loan agreements, for example). These new contractual forms reflect the influence of Anglo-Saxon legal traditions. Internationalization of the economy further complicates these patterns of circulation and contracting, requiring parties to reach beyond the usual legal models for doing business. Both pose many challenges for judicial systems, some of which are outlined below:

- *To respond rapidly* to the conflicts that these new forms of economic exchange inevitably entail. The challenge to respond quickly involves systems of financing, budgeting, and using resources in the judicial system, as well as adequate procedural systems.
- *To respond adequately* to the new type of litigation. Those who participate in resolving conflicts, as mediators, lawyers, or judges, require certain kinds of knowledge. A minimum understanding is needed of the language and characteristics of the economic and financial arena in which the conflict arose. This means new types of judicial specialization and training, which are already beginning in various countries of Central America, as well as in Colombia, Chile, Peru, Bolivia, and Argentina.

Judges also need a minimum understanding of the economic processes affected by their decisions, so as to take responsibility for the effects of their decisions. Even where judges must make decisions based upon legal or moral principles and not based on some calculus of well-being or efficiency, they can hardly render judgements without considering their economic consequences. Similarly the internationalization of the economy poses challenges to legal training and specialization.

Understanding the bases and principles of other judicial systems is important, especially as principles or concepts from other legal systems begin to intersect with our own. The internationalized economy will increasingly require the application of foreign law, and this presents challenges in legal training and specialization.

• *To respond with flexibility* to the growing diversity of legal forms and conflicts. It does not seem reasonable that the state provide only the traditional judicial response of strict application of the law to such diverse conflicts and forms. Particularly in litigation between parties that intend to continue working together, alternative forms of conflict resolution could aim not only at assigning responsibilities, but also at maintaining collaboration between the parties. These objectives typically are better achieved through channels such as mediation than through judicial decisions. Thus, for example, in Argentina and Colombia alternative dispute resolution mechanisms (ADR) have been promoted. These mechanisms are attracting strong interest in most countries of the region, and are being advanced by agencies such as the U.S. Agency for International Development.

Redefining the Role of the State

Democratization and modernization processes are also redefining the size and role of the state, reducing government's capacity to intervene, but affirming its regulatory powers. It is taken for granted that the protection of rights and promotion of well-being are better pursued by setting rules than by implementing government programs. For the judiciary, this means more litigation and greater importance attributed to its work. Already the judicial branch has increased its importance in relation to the executive branch. In addition, and more importantly, this shift comes about because the success of governmental or community development programs implemented through rule-making depends fundamentally on the effectiveness of such rules themselves, which in turn depends largely on the capacity of the judiciary to punish noncompliance and resolve conflicts arising out of such rules. A weak judiciary not only means impunity for violators of the norms, but also that their violations will probably increase, so long as the general preventive effect is not operative.

Strengthening of regulatory power raises the need, first, to respond to the sharp increase in litigation generated by the expanded regulatory role of the state; and, second, to strengthen the judicial systems, as an essential requirement for maintaining the social legitimacy of liberal democracy. The advent of a more liberal economic and political system shifts the population's attention from the political institutions that create order to those that interpret and apply it. No longer is the question of which is the most appropriate economic or political order a topic of discussion; the most relevant debate occurs in interpreting this order, not replacing it, as typically occurred during the first three quarters of this century. Upon the deregulation of economic and social activity, the actors seek not so much to change the rules, but to attempt to see to it that the most generic and stable concepts are interpreted in a manner that benefits their interests. Likewise, social demands are less geared to transforming the economic system or the political order and more to the fulfillment of promises of well-being and freedom. These demands for carrying out promises are often directed at the judiciary. For example, in Costa Rica, Argentina, Colombia, Chile, and Mexico, litigation has increased significantly in the last two decades.

Moreover, it appears reasonable to think that the discussion about redefining the role and size of the state will sooner or later produce an in-depth debate on the role and the size of the judicial system. The classic response concerning the judicial function has its origins in constitutional process and codification, according to which the judiciary should resolve every legally significant conflict, protect every right violated, and punish every violation of the law. This response no longer holds weight. Due to limited resources, it has become impossible for the judiciary to carry out a wide range of functions. Yet Latin American judicial systems have long refused to establish selective criteria for accepting the cases most important to society. Consequently other forces have made this selection, with effects that violate certain basic principles or basic rights, and, in many cases, severely impair the efficiency of the system.

In the area of criminal law as well, many judicial systems have been overloaded with less important cases, losing the capacity to judge the most serious crimes. This has led to a series of distortions, such as, for example, having had to delegate some judicial functions to bodies such as the ministry of justice or the police. (Examples of this may be found in Argentina, Venezuela, and Peru.) In other cases, the necessity to fill the void where the state should act has been taken up by private actors who are limited in their ability to guarantee due process (such as the *rondas campesinas*, or peasant patrols, in Peru). As a result, many were convinced of the need to apply a selective criterion according to principles of reason through the principle of opportunity; this criterion has begun to take hold. The reforms of the code of criminal procedure and in the justice ministry in various countries of the region have addressed this objective of selectivity.

In the civil jurisdiction, the market has typically had the role of establishing restrictions on entry to the judicial system, which is detrimental to the more marginal groups, while placing state resources at the disposal of the wealthiest, free of charge.

Challenges to Judicial Systems

Redefining the size and role of government poses two types of challenges to judicial systems. First is the need to establish, as clearly as possible, the role or function of the judiciary. Second is the challenge to diversify governmental responses to these social conflicts that the judicial system ought to resolve, but which in fact do not reach it.

Selectiveness

Because judicial systems cannot solve all the legally significant problems of society, the scarce resources of the judiciary must be available for the problems of greatest social import and those most susceptible to judicial resolution. Then we must find and employ alternatives to the judiciary: for example, preventing legal conflicts through formal and informal education. Another solution is to refer conflicts with the lowest judicial component to the intervention of a justice of the peace or administrative agents under the law, or to state agencies outside the judicial realm. Interested parties can be offered the option to refer matters to a court if they become litigious. This could occur typically with matters involving voluntary jurisdiction and executory matters. (In Colombia one finds the greatest efforts and proposals for extrajudicial settlement of disputes. In Chile, this tendency is in its early stages.) A third solution is to strengthen alternative dispute resolution mechanisms, such as mediation, arbitration, and conciliation.

Recognition of Cultural Diversity

Democratization and modernization processes typically produce more open societies, in terms of ethnicity, gender, and lifestyle. This heterogeneity tends to bring an increase in litigation involving morally complex problems, in the area of family law, divorce, communities of homosexuals, lawsuits for recognition of ethnic identities, and the like. To respond appropriately to this challenge, judges need training and continuing education to strengthen their capacity to engage in moral argument, without attempting to impose a single model. Many of these issues, especially in family law, suggest flexible responses that go beyond the simple application of legal principles, typically based on assigning responsibilities, rights, and obligations. The delicate moral issues involved and the need for parties to work together, especially in the case of family conflicts, are more appropriately handled by methods of mediation and conflict resolution than by judicial decision-making.

Additionally, the process of cultural modernization in our societies tends to undermine many structures that once could function spontaneously to prevent conflicts or bring about solutions. Thus, the destruction of extended family structures, the rural-urban migration, the diaspora of indigenous communities, and other similar phenomena, have eliminated means of preventing or resolving conflicts within families or neighborhoods. This helps to explain the significant increase in litigation in many countries in the region. Again, this situation cannot be addressed by merely increasing the number of courts, which typically occurred in the 1980s in countries such as Argentina, Chile, Colombia, and Mexico. Instead, the challenge seems to lie in diversifying the state's responses, reserving the judicial option for conflicts that clearly require it, and assuring the maximum "social utility" of investments to improve the justice systems.

Modernization of Judicial Management

The modernization of productive processes, which has brought with it economic liberalization, has required the modification of state administrative practices in order to adapt the state to the new conditions of national and international competition. Thus, efficiency criteria based on administrative methods used in the private sector have been introduced to public administration. Efficiency in the public sector is defined in terms of public good, of course, whereas private sector objectives have to do with maximizing profit, but the techniques are easily adapted to new purposes. Thus, the public sector agencies are increasingly scrutinized for their efficiency, social utility, optimal use of resources, targeting of expenditures, etc. This reform usually begins in the executive branch, at the urging of ministers of finance. Economists in the development field (typically U.S.-trained and encouraged by international organizations) have made substantial contributions to this process.

In the last five years, the judicial systems in Latin America have also been facing these new challenges. They are requested to answer whether the investment made by taxpayers in the judiciary is being utilized and administered in a way that guarantees optimal delivery of the service of justice to the population. The issue of court administration and allocation of resources has met with responses involving structural changes in countries such as Colombia, Costa Rica, Uruguay, Argentina, and Chile.

The challenge of modernizing judicial systems along the lines indicated requires that we give serious attention to a number of concerns, ranging from public information to resource allocation.

Public Awareness and Information

In the first place, the public must be made aware that modernizing judicial systems constitutes a major challenge, which does not simply entail supplying each judge's office with a word processor. Modernization of the judiciary requires an objective and empirical evaluation of how judicial systems function, their degree of efficiency, and the resources they use. This evaluation, in turn, requires taking significant steps in areas traditionally very backward in the countries of the region.

First, to produce this evaluation, it is necessary to collect data to construct useful and reliable statistics. (Such statistics are unreliable in virtually the entire region, particularly in Central America except for Costa Rica, and in Peru, Paraguay, and Argentina). At the same time, it is necessary to strengthen interdisciplinary networks that may help to describe the efficiencies and inefficiencies of the judicial system, to which end lawyers need to be brought together with systems engineers and managers. (This is already under way in Colombia and is beginning to pick up steam in Chile).

Analysis of Data

Latin American countries have not developed a stable legal academic profession. The region's universities tend to value formal knowledge of law over information based on investigating reality or evaluating legal policies. Instead, governments and some non-governmental organizations, often doing without the university sector, have taken on the task of forming and building teams capable of describing the operations of the judicial sector and recommending appropriate public policies to improve its performance. Examples of this include the Instituto S.E.R. of Colombia, ILANUD in Costa Rica; for Central America, Florida International University; the Instituto de Derecho Procesal in Uruguay; and in Chile, the Ministry of Justice, Universidad Diego Portales, and Corporación de Promoción Universitaria.

Planning and Administering Resources

To achieve this goal, several judicial systems in the region have created administrative offices within the judiciary with the capacity to prepare budget proposals and to administer their resources with autonomously. (Examples are to be found in Costa Rica, Colombia, Argentina, and Chile.) However, this task still needs support and a firmer definition regarding the extent of autonomy that the judicial branch should have to administer its own resources, so as to strike a balance between its need for independence and the need to coordinate financial matters among the various state entities.

Monitoring and Incentives for Resource Allocation

The judiciary is a branch of government that is very sensitive regarding its functional independence. Nonetheless, the fact that it administers public funds calls for some level of outside control, which requires evaluation systems. The most complex systems are required to evaluate the performance of judges, who should enjoy full independence in carrying out their tasks. Keeping this objective in mind, a set of incentives and sanctions should be adopted to strengthen the performance of judges. These systems should be introduced to the career service regime of judges, where one exists. While it is extremely difficult to measure the amount and quality of a judge's work, certain indicators can be effective, if used with appropriate flexibility.

Citizen Power

The processes of democratization and modernization of Latin American societies have included the demand for the state to be capable of responding to the needs of its citizens with diligence, equity, and transparency, and to follow through appropriately on the promises of freedom and well-being made by the state itself, whether through human rights that are protected in constitutional texts or through rights that are recognized in statutes. The democratization process has been understood in the 1990s to include some peculiarities that are manifested with special intensity. The notion of democratic society that is coming to prevail demands the strengthening of civil society, of its intermediate organizations, especially those reaching the most disadvantaged or marginal. With greater equality in the competition for resources and in the political and social dialogue, the various groups should have sufficient power and capacity to be able to influence public fora and the organization of the state. This goes along with the notion that the state is more a service organization than a center of power; in this regard, emphasis had been placed on the fact that it is a public power. From this we may infer that one of the principal characteristics of a modern democracy is that the citizens may demand of the state that it carry out its tasks, requiring accessibility, transparency in its actions, and efficiency in the manner in which it achieves its objectives. It is here that the notion arises that the state entity should be subject to oversight by citizens.

The phenomenon described above is now beginning to reach the judicial systems. They now face a series of challenges that consist, first, of the need for efficiency and transparency in the operation of the judicial system, and second, of the judiciary being capable of ensuring that the other institutions act transparently and according to the law.

In light of the first challenge, there is a need to seek and demonstrate efficiency in the use of the public resources invested in justice, a topic which was addressed above. Another result is a growing demand for transparency from the judicial system, which implies the challenge of reducing to a minimum the risks of corruption, political clientelism, or internal corporatism. Creating institutional designs capable of eliminating the growing influence of these factors and guaranteeing that those that are latent do not interfere are especially complex tasks. The history of the judicial systems of the region has been marked by constant political

interventions, leading to political party clientelism and obedience to the government in office at the time, which are incompatible with the idea of a strong, independent judiciary capable of keeping a check on the other organs of the state and
the groups with the greatest influence or power in society. (This is the case, for
example, in most of the Central American countries, excluding Costa Rica, and in
Venezuela and Peru). Where political intervention has been more tenuous or has
been limited in general to replacing members of the Supreme Court (as in Argentina), or where it has been sporadic or rare (as in Chile), a strong corporatist
spirit has arisen among the judges, resulting in a lack of transparency and in clientelistic relations among judges as a professional group. It should be noted that
this clientelism has created de facto judicial career systems, or helped to strengthen
them, and has served to decrease the risks of corruption, or to maintain it at
relatively low levels. Nonetheless, the same corporatism has tended to isolate the
judicial profession from the political sectors and social demands, which has made
it difficult for the judges to adapt to the changes or to understand the social demands for change, which they typically interpret as unjust attacks that ignore
their reality.

The challenge, then, is to ensure the maximum independence of the judiciary, so long as it coordinates with the other branches of government, and that is
attuned to societal requirements, and operates with utmost transparency. To this
end, mechanisms are needed to check the activities of the judges to ensure they
attend to these concerns, without violating their necessary autonomy. This should
be considered not only in the legal regulation of how judges are appointed, permanent tenure in office for judges, removal for political trial or for criminal or
administrative liability, systems of qualifications, the structuring of the judicial
career, and other regulations that typically have been understood as part of this
topic; but, also, it is necessary to analyze in depth the transparency of judicial
processes, the conditions that enable and oblige judges to give reasoned justifica-
tions for their decisions and take responsibility for building public knowledge,
and criticism of the work of the judiciary.

These characteristics particular to democracies, which demand the strengthening of civil society and of its capacity to submit a state institution to oversight,
also pose the challenge of monitoring the legal quality of the actions of the state
and of the powerful groups in society. One of the key instruments democracies
have to keep the institutions of the state in line with the law is precisely that the
citizens may demand the fulfillment of these responsibilities in the courts. There
are also non-traditional mechanisms for demanding these rights, such as actions
in the public interest and for the protection of diffuse collective rights. For the
judiciary to be able to respond to these demands, not only is it necessary to review the efficiency, internal transparency, and independence of the judiciary. It is
also necessary to think seriously about other mechanisms capable of ensuring

the courts are sufficiently strong. These include, in addition to those already mentioned regarding independence, the necessity for in-depth review of the resources that the state allocates to the functioning of the system, which have traditionally been scarce, even when there is a growing trend to increase the budgets of the judicial branches and to assure, by constitutional provisions, that they receive at least a given percentage of state resources. This increase in resources demands that the judiciary, in turn, be capable of making optimal use of them through efficient management.

Conclusion

In summary, the economic, social, and cultural transformations under way in Latin America pose not only quantitative requirements, but also challenges that call for clear assessments. Various assumptions by which we traditionally constructed and evaluated judicial systems are no longer valid. Without the history or the cultural base of the European societies, we accepted the ideals of constitutionalism and codification, and the resulting institutions never closely resembled the stated ideals in their actual functioning.

The roles in the judicial system must now be redefined, taking into account the limits of available resources. We must tackle the issue of independence, following a not very felicitous history in this regard. Above all, those elements that would strengthen the judiciary must be recognized, and that is linked to meeting the challenges arising from modernization and democratization in Latin America.

PART III

INTERNATIONAL COOPERATION IN JUDICIAL REFORM

CHAPTER 12

Regional Integration and Convergence of Legal Systems

Miguel Rodríguez

Approaches to development have always varied across Latin America, as have strategies and modes of regional integration. Today, however, economic liberalization in the Latin American and Caribbean countries is giving new meaning and importance to regional coalitions. The old view that trade liberalization was incompatible with regional integration efforts no longer holds. The region's economies are adjusting to the rigors of competition, and at the same time, reinforcing the processes of integration that will improve their participation in the global economy.

During the 1960s and 1970s, ambitious regional and subregional plans at integration failed again and again, due to economic policies that made them impossible. How could one integrate countries that gave preference to their own internal markets, if opening up to neighboring markets was the very basis for integration? When "inward-oriented" development strategies were protecting national industries, it made no sense to allow competition from other countries.

After the mid 1980s, a radical change ensued. In response to economic crises and foreign debt problems, various countries began to adopt policies for structural adjustment and economic modernization that radically transformed their development strategies. Protectionism was replaced by trade liberalization policies, and the central focus moved from the internal market to the global market. Export promotion policies displaced import substitution. Efficiency and competitiveness became a necessary condition of the industrialization processes.

These new directions had a decisive impact on attempts at regional integration. Mercosur and the Andean Group became two of the first and most successful free trade areas in the developing world, and are now moving toward becoming customs unions. Other examples include the reactivation of the Central American Common Market; changes in Caricom; the Group of Three agreement; Chile's trade agreements with Mexico, Colombia, and Venezuela; agreements that Venezuela and Colombia have with Caricom and Central America; and the present negotiations by Chile and the Andean Group countries with Mercosur.

These efforts are aimed at establishing free trade areas or customs unions among the participating countries. While they may not be perfectly coordinated, they are setting the stage for a great Latin American economic zone, free of restrictions on the flow of goods, services, and investment, in which the region's countries can sustain their economic development and simultaneously meet the enormous challenges of participating in the global economy. Added to this are expectations for a free trade area of the Americas, in which the developed North and the developing South could establish a new framework for cooperation and understanding on economic matters.

The New Latin American Integration

We are witnessing a new concept of Latin American integration, with at least four distinct characteristics. First, economic liberalization is one of the characteristic features. The attempts to integrate the countries of the region behind a protectionist wall have been abandoned. By changing their traditional economic policy orientation and discontinuing import substitution strategies, the countries also abandoned what could be called the "planned" concept of integration, and adopted an integration strategy based on a trade opening "inwards" within the subregions, and outwardly from the subregions. There are no closed trading blocs among our countries; the subregional arrangements have become facilitators of the opening. The convergence of these arrangements, with a view to forming a Latin American economic zone and a hemispheric free trade agreement, is perhaps the best evidence of the concept of "opening" central to the new Latin American integration.

Second, business people, not governments, are the leading players of the new Latin American integration. The "administrative" and "bureaucratic" management of the integration process is a thing of the past. Business people are no longer spectators to integration, but have become its principal impetus. It is the private sector in Latin America that is giving concrete meaning to efforts to integrate the region.

In joining the integration process, Latin American businesses are now discovering the value of neighboring markets and taking advantage of trade and investment opportunities that are opening up with the deepening of integration. The dynamism of commercial transactions in recent years among Brazil, Uruguay, and Argentina, and between Colombia and Venezuela, are examples. Even more significant is the large flow of intraregional investment, which is unprecedented in the economic history of Latin America.

Third, the new Latin American integration has taken many forms. It is an unorthodox integration. There is no one model of integration being implemented. Varying forms of closer ties among the countries coexist, each based on the particular circumstances and interests in question. At present there are four agreements among Latin American countries aimed at forming customs unions (the Andean Group, Mercosur, Caricom, and the CACM), and 12 agreements to establish free trade areas, not including the numerous agreements of partial scope signed under the framework of ALADI. Most of the countries are members of one or another subregional integration arrangement with their neighbors. However, at the same time, many countries are participating in bilateral agreements aimed at forming free trade areas among the participants. In general, these differing modalities share a common objective: to foster more extensive economic linkages among the countries of the region, through accelerated programs for the reciprocal elimination of restrictions on trade and investment. In a way, expanding foreign markets, which goes hand-in-hand with the "outward-oriented" growth strategies now practiced by the countries of the region, is aimed mainly at opening up the Latin American markets.

Finally, the new Latin American integration may be termed "programmatic." Unlike the past, integration efforts are based on automatic free trade programs that encompass the world of tariffs and duties, and whose purpose is to eliminate trade restrictions in a very short time, thereby creating conditions for a rapid increase in trade flows among the countries of the region.

Here again, the influence of the processes of economic liberalization undertaken by the Latin American countries have been determinant, for insofar as these countries have unilaterally opened up their economies to the rest of the world, it makes no sense to exclude certain products or sectors from the liberalization programs agreed upon with other countries of the region, as was the case in the past. In fact, the intra-Latin American agreements aim to accelerate trade liberalization, more so than in other regions, without making it more selective.

Economic Integration and Legal Systems

The legal systems in place in Latin America are profoundly affected by this kind of integration, based upon the opening of trade with private economic actors actively participating. Influenced by the institutional framework of subregional and bilateral trade and integration agreements, national legal systems are undergoing change. A progressive convergence of the legal systems of the region is taking place with the adoption of market institutions and the transformation of legal codes, to bring them into line with the free trade disciplines essential to new development strategies and integration arrangements.

In effect, the transition from economies subject to state intervention, to market economies, is ushering in a radical transformation of the national legal codes. These changes have ensured that in most cases government is no longer the principal source of primary regulation, and legislatures are increasingly taking the initiative to adapt and expand the countries' economic legislation. In general, transforming the legal systems has involved the task of unifying the law around the values proposed by economic competition.

It is a sign of new times. In an open economy, the private sector assumes a leading role in economic development and the law should respond to this reality, creating an adequate environment for economic actors to make more independent decisions, geared to a more global market. Most countries of the region have introduced new legislation regarding free competition, consumer protection, investment, protection of intellectual property rights, and regulation of unfair trade practices, to mention the most important issues.

This new legal and institutional framework should enable the private sector to anticipate investment opportunities with better predictability; help policymakers to give more rational direction to investment; and make it easier for public administrators and judges to guarantee the effective enforcement of the rules of the game that sustain the market economy. In this environment, law enforcement in the region has less opportunity for abuses of power, thereby giving stability and legal security to those involved in economic activities.

From the perspective of integration, the revitalization of subregional arrangements during a time of economic liberalization raises old problems—such as the harmonization of legislation, the enforcement of rules derived from the agreements, and, in general, building institutions able to consolidate and further the advantages of integration. As regional integration proceeds, the question of leveling conditions of competition in the integrated areas arises. By "leveling" the conditions of competition, I mean a legal and institutional framework that avoids awarding undue advantages to one country's economic actors at the expense of other countries.

In this context, the defense of competition requires decisive action by the state both internally and externally. Internally, it means enforcing rules to prevent the establishment of monopolies or the abuse of dominant market positions. Therefore, the countries are committed to deterring economic concentrations whose purpose is to limit or restrict competition so as to set production conditions and prices. In recent years, countries such as Mexico, Argentina, Brazil, Colombia, and Venezuela have adopted laws to protect or promote competition. Externally, the defense of competition entails protecting national industry from damages caused by imports of dumped or state-subsidized goods. Trade opening means that local production is subjected to international competition, which can improve efficiency and competitiveness; however, this must exclude unfair trade practices such as dumping and subsidies. Consequently, economic liberalization has also produced measures to control unfair trade practices, particularly anti-dumping and countervailing duties imposed by many of the countries in the region, such as Mexico, Chile, Colombia, and Venezuela. So a close relationship exists between economic liberalization and integration, and legislative require-ments, for both new laws and amendments to existing ones.

Eventually, the convergence of different integration agreements, as well as the proposed free trade area of the Americas, will require new law and new insti-tutions. In this scenario, clauses to protect trade, rules for classifying the origin of merchandise, protection of intellectual property rights, and dispute settlement mechanisms, among others, should be accorded harmonized treatment resulting from the adoption and implementation of rules shared by all countries of the region.

Progress towards higher stages of integration will undoubtedly call for a legal and institutional framework common to all the countries of the region, in which elements of supranationality progressively replace the national sphere. We are moving in that direction; much has already been accomplished, but much remains to be done.

CHAPTER 13

The World Bank

Ibrahim Shihata

A legal system consists not only of a set of legal rules and regulations, but also of the processes for applying and enforcing those rules and the various means for resolving legal disputes. The World Bank's experience in the area of judicial reform, while it remains limited, has yielded certain findings regarding legal systems in this broader sense. After describing various ways in which the Bank supports judicial reform in its member countries, this paper will outline the general principles that, according to the Bank's experience, are essential to reform of justice systems.

Instruments to Assist Judicial Reform

Assistance to judicial reform programs in its borrowing countries is offered by the World Bank to promote a stable business environment in which investment for productive purposes may expand and prosper. In this context, judicial reform is a critical element of any comprehensive reform, necessary to strengthen the rule of law and the state's role as its guarantor. For this reason, judicial reform should go hand in hand with legal, regulatory and administrative reforms. Each of these depends for its success or failure on the others. The emphasis on judicial reform, therefore, should not divert attention from the importance of carrying out simultaneous reforms in the legal and administrative fields.

World Bank assistance is provided through a number of financial instruments, including adjustment loans, investment loans, institutional development grants, and diagnostic studies in preparation for lending activities. Under *adjustment loans*, which support policy reforms through the financing of general imports, the Bank has agreed with certain countries on actions affecting the judiciary. These include studies of the current state of a country's judiciary, coupled with steps to improve court administration or the judiciary's role in applying new laws and regulations. Adjustment loans have also focused on specific actions involving courts, and even the establishment of new courts to assist in settling disputes over investment and commercial activities, particularly disputes between commercial banks and their borrowers. Adjustment loans are meant to be quick-disbursing, however, and thus are typically suited for short-term reforms. A series of adjustment loans to the same country could nevertheless address reforms implementable over a longer term if their scope and sequencing were identified from the start.

For judicial reform measures over a longer period of two to five years, the main vehicles for World Bank assistance are *investment operations*, especially institution-building and technical assistance loans. These aim at improving the effectiveness of the judiciary, especially in enforcing private sector transactions and in promoting transparency and accountability of government actions—factors that are highly relevant to our objective of facilitating and promoting private investment.

Our activities in judicial reform have also involved *in-depth studies* of a country's judiciary to assess reform needs for the better administration of justice. These studies have been done either by Bank staff in economic and sector work, as in Ecuador, Peru and Trinidad and Tobago, or through grants to governments (such as Argentina) from funds (such as the Institutional Development Fund established in 1992), or bilateral grant programs which the Bank executes.

Supporting judicial reform is a relatively new area of involvement for the World Bank, and it poses special challenges due to its cultural, economic, political and legal factors. As the Bank is engaged in a learning process in this area, this account simply outlines some lessons we have learned in assisting borrowing countries in the design, preparation and implementation of judicial reform programs.

Many of the judicial reform components of Bank investment loans with broader objectives, as well as self-standing technical assistance operations directed at the judiciary, are preceded by in-depth surveys and research. Thorough diagnostic work has been critical in identifying the specific issues and problems in the justice systems of particular countries, and in designing meaningful reform programs. The Bank's detailed review in 1994 of Ecuador's judicial sector is an example of a study that provided a useful analysis of major issues affecting the judiciary.

The issues discussed in that study are common to many countries. Projects now underway in Venezuela and Bolivia address similar questions. The Bank also has self-standing projects under preparation in Ecuador, Peru, Albania and Poland, and judicial reform components in technical assistance loans in other countries.

Preliminary Findings

Whether a country follows Roman civil law traditions, common law, Islamic Shari'a or another legal system, the steps to be taken in identifying problems in the administration of justice do not vary greatly. When gathering information for the diagnostic studies, it is important to interview and collect materials from many sources: judges at all levels of courts; court administrators and officials at justice ministries; judicial academies and training institutes; members of bar associations and law firms; law school professors and legal scholars; representatives of local and foreign business communities, including chambers of commerce; members of judiciary committees in parliaments, if any; and non-governmental organizations. In addition, there may be country-specific institutions, such as law reform commissions that are instrumental for any diagnostic process. One example is the Institute of Planning (Bapenas) in Indonesia, which is heavily involved in the country's legal reforms.

The conceptual framework used by Bank staff to analyze issues related to the administration of justice and to distinguish between efficient and inefficient justice systems, is based on certain principles described below.

The administration of justice is essentially a service delivered by the state to the community, in order to maintain social peace and harmony and facilitate economic and social development through the resolution of legal disputes that arise in the community. The ultimate beneficiary of the justice system and of judicial reform is the society at large. The purpose of reform is to enable the judiciary to serve affected parties, including the economic agents in the society, efficiently and fairly.

A main obstacle to the efficient administration of justice, and to trade, investment, and economic development in general, is the gap between the law as enacted, and the behavior of society and the economy in practice. This gap is more pronounced in less developed countries. While the public often finds ways to compensate for this gap (e.g., through informal sectors or black markets), the judge is inevitably confronted with it and must bridge it through his rulings in the specific cases presented to him.

How judges respond to this challenge is critical for developing an efficient system of justice administration. In many developing countries, the machinery of justice is not adequately prepared to face this challenge, and cannot fulfill its role of maintaining social peace and facilitating economic development through the resolution of existing disputes and the avoidance and resolution of future ones. As a result of this and other factors, the community's confidence in the legal system as a whole and in specific legislation is critically low in those countries.

Such situations can hardly be reversed simply through financial resources provided by the Bank or other sources to carry out reform and to obtain political support to change existing legislation. Opposition from a leading group of judges and the core of the legal community could easily bring a fully funded reform program to a halt. Hence, the importance of the participation of the judiciary and the local legal profession in the reform projects.

Finally, in analyzing the justice system, it is also necessary to visit the actual places, offices and buildings where judges and courts operate in order to appreciate how the system works in real life and determine whether the actual physical facilities and working methods are conducive to an efficient administration of justice.

Main Issues in Judicial Reform

With the above findings in mind, the starting point for the Bank to evaluate and identify problems in the judicial system of a given country has been to examine the following elements:

a) the legal framework of the country and the role of judges within this framework;
b) position of judges in society and the perception of the system of administration of justice by the community;
c) the integrity of the justice system;
d) the administration of the judicial system;
e) the economic cost of justice in the country;
f) access to justice;
g) the availability of legal information;
h) legal education and training;
I) the actual functioning of legal procedures;
j) physical facilities of courts;
k) the impact of court decisions on society; and
l) alternative dispute resolution mechanisms.

Legal Framework and the Role of Judges

The context for operations of the justice system includes not only political, economic and social factors—which are extremely important—but the overall legal framework as well. The legal context can make a dramatic difference in the real meaning of legal norms and their perception by the society, even without considering their actual implementation and effectiveness. By way of example, in the former legal system of Soviet Russia, the civil code provisions dealing with succession, wills and inheritance did not differ significantly from those common in Western Europe or the United States. Radical differences appeared only when these provisions were combined with the property law provisions of the same code, which gave strong preference to state property and assumed its prevalence.

The gap between the law as written and the law as applied is common in many societies. At times it results from the convenience of applying the law in innovative ways, rather than seeking its amendment. But in many developing countries, law is somewhat disconnected from public opinion. Sometimes the written

law does not reflect general moral convictions in the community, or is not perceived as serving community interests. Ordinary citizens may find their way around
this problem, and public officials may apply the law according to the circumstances. Judges, however, are expected to apply the written law, a daunting task
in the context where social practice is different.

An important element of the legal context is the analysis of how the role of
the judiciary is defined within that context. Related to this is an analysis of the
expectations placed on the judge with respect to the interpretation and application of the law in specific disputes. Obviously, the expectations of common law
systems differ substantially from those based on civil law traditions. Yet both
systems operate on the basis of the principle that a judge may not bring in a finding of *non liquet*. In common law countries, judges may have acquired a de facto
lawmaking function. In civil law jurisdictions, judges occasionally fill the lacunae
left by legislators through broad "interpretative" decisions.

Certain additional points worth mentioning are the adequacy of the sources
of law to allow judges to fulfill their role; problems of legal language and termi-
nology, including problems in the use of legal classifications; organization of the
courts; organization of the legal profession; and the system of legal education.

Position of Judges and Community Perceptions of the Justice System

An important element of a functioning judicial system is the position of judges in
the society, their independence and security. The independence of the judiciary is
a means to achieve impartial, fair and efficient judgments. It is usually achieved
through constitutionally enshrined principles coupled with legislative guarantees
of independence and non-interference from the executive and legislative branches of government. In addition to constitutional guarantees, elements of judicial
independence usually include the tenure of judges, salary scales set by law, guaranteeing of personal and financial security by the state, and strictly prescribed
procedures for the removal of judges from office. In real life, however, the independence of the judiciary is embedded in the country's tradition and history and
is often associated with the degree of its political and social development.

The independence of judges is not to be equated to their isolation from the
forces which influence behavior in their societies. It does not mean that judges
ought to treat law as a set of rigid rules insulated from the forces which brought
them to being and those which emerged since their adoption. Such blind application of the law, at times defended under the banner of judicial independence,
tends to marginalize the role of courts, and eventually the law itself.

The administration of justice is a service provided, principally, by the state
to society. In order to evaluate how the service is delivered, it is necessary to ask
the actors and users how they perceive it: how judges perceive their own func-

tion and the general conditions of the job; how lawyers in law firms and bar associations, academics, and other legal scholars perceive the judicial system; and how the ultimate users, including business people and ordinary citizens, view the justice system. It is they who will give a true and final testimony of how the service is working, and whether the courts are independent, efficient, prompt, inexpensive and effective.

Some judges contend that the loser in a lawsuit tends to blame the courts for the outcome. But any analyst is bound to take that into account. The paradox that we face in some developing countries is that not only the losing parties complain, but also the successful litigants, since many of the judicial victories are only paper triumphs which, insulated from the economic, moral, social and political forces at play, become devoid of any legal content.

Integrity of the System

The extent to which a justice system is subject to corruption imposes additional costs on the society and leads to further inefficiencies in the administration of justice. Corruption also frustrates the legitimate expectations and trust of the public. It is important to determine what the causes of corruption are and whether they can be eliminated through a judicial reform program or, as is often the case, through more far-reaching measures, by reducing restrictions and discretionary exceptions, and increasing transparency and accountability.

Administration and Management

Another aspect that needs to be analyzed is the administrative structure that should enable the machinery of justice to work effectively. In our experience, one of the most prevalent features of the justice systems in developing countries around the world is the lack or weakness of administrative support and organization for judges at every level. A proper administration of the system often requires a careful examination of the following points:

- *Management of the judiciary sector*, namely the determination of jurisdictions geographically and by subject matter; determination of number of courts and judges by population and number of cases; and planning and development of the judiciary.
- *Personnel issues*, namely selection and appointment of judges; level of judges' salaries; incentives and promotion of judges; independence and tenure of judges; accountability of judges and codes of ethics; discipline, sanctions, and removal of judges; as well as the appointment, promotion, discipline, and removal of judicial support staff.

- *Interrelations of the judiciary* with the executive, the legislature, bar associations and other professional bodies and the press, including ethical issues of conflict of interest which may arise in the context of such relationships.
- *Case management*, namely, assignment of cases; case load; flow of cases through the court procedure; management of hearings, gathering and production of evidence, and oral and written arguments; writing of decisions; and organization of a judge's work.

Economic Costs of Justice

The fourth aspect to be examined is the economic costs that the administration of justice represents for the society. One needs to distinguish between costs resulting from the functioning of a generally efficient judiciary and additional costs imposed on society by inefficiencies and arbitrariness. By the former we mean the relation between the costs and benefits of the system, the rationality of the cost structure, and how much of the cost is distributed between the general tax payer base and the direct users of the system (litigants). Pertinent points in this respect include:

- the economic cost of justice to the state, namely the percentage of the national budget allocated to the judiciary; distribution of expenses within the judiciary's budget; administration of the budget (initiative, approval, decisions and responsibility); and budget control;
- the economic cost of justice to the litigants, namely court fees and lawyers' fees;
- incidental expenses and legal aid, if any; and
- the economic cost of justice to the society—mostly the indirect cost, to be identified through an analysis of how corruption and the lack of transparent and predictable rules result in increased arbitrariness of the system, excessive appeals and reviews.

Access to Justice

An important element of an equitable judicial system is access to courts. Access to justice is affected by several factors, including the geographic and subject distribution of courts, confidence in the system, the availability of translation facilities for litigants, the degree of understanding of litigants' rights, civic education, the complexity of procedures required for filing a claim, and court fees and costs. The last element can have a profound impact on the volume of submitted claims. In some jurisdictions, the level of court fees is successfully used as a deterrent against frivolous claims. However, that the same fees that discourage unnecessary litigation can also prevent access to courts by large portions of the population. An efficient and equitable administration of justice, therefore, requires balancing these two competing interests. Providing legal aid to the poor who have prima facie legitimate claims helps the justice system to address this issue.

Availability of Legal Information

In many developing countries, laws and regulations generally applicable to the population are published in limited quantities, with great delay, or not published at all. In some francophone African countries, official gazettes have not been published for several years. In certain remote provinces of Russia, judges have been reported to apply laws that are no longer in force, due to the lack of dissemination of newly promulgated laws. Such situations can cause judges to render unfair judgments, and generally contribute to increased appeals and a state of legal uncertainty. In countries that follow the common law tradition, it is also important to make court judgments available in a timely and readily accessible manner.

In addition to laws, regulations and court decisions, reliable court statistics are often hard to locate in developing countries. Without such information, it is difficult to design a reform program to address the problems of court administration and case management.

Legal Education and Training

Apart from the insufficiencies which may exist in the administration and management of the justice systems, judicial education and training is usually one of the weakest points in the delivery of justice in developing and transition countries. This is not limited to education in various areas of substantive law and court procedures for judges. Equally, if not more, important is the necessity to: (i) raise the judges' consciousness about the need for modernization of the system and improving the methodology of administration of justice and (ii) instill in the judiciary a culture of service in which the judge is not the central figure of the system, but rather a servant of the society for efficient dispute resolution. Related to this is the need to train the judges in judicial reasoning and the exercise of judicial discretion. This is especially important in the countries of transition where, under the previous regime, judges were frequently mere executors of state policies, regardless of the interests of the litigants.

While the change in attitudes is crucial, it is also important to ensure that judges (both early in their legal education at universities and as part of continuing legal education) will be trained in complex areas of economic and commercial law, such as laws and regulations governing banking transactions, corporations, capital markets and securities, insurance, transport, finance, trade in intangibles, anti-trust, intellectual property, consumer protection, and economic crimes. The lack of knowledge of new laws and regulations can be seriously detrimental to the effectiveness of judicial dispute resolution. This is particularly true in the economies in transition where the volume of new legislation (even assuming that judges have access to the newest enactments) contributes to great delays in the resolution of disputes.

Training, of course, should not be limited to the judges, but must include all those involved in the administration of justice. A special problem in developing countries is the frequent lack of training for support staff and court personnel.

How Legal Procedures Actually Function

The court procedures in developing countries, including the distribution of cases, pleadings, hearings, and the writing of decisions, are often outdated and contribute to the inefficiency of the justice system. As a result, they do not keep up with the need for a speedy resolution of disputes and thus add to the inefficiencies in the justice system. Cumbersome court procedures, such as excessive formal prerequisites, also decrease the accessibility of the justice system to the general population.

The relevance of procedure to a proper administration of justice can be readily discerned in the following areas:

Distribution of Cases. A crucial aspect to examine is how individual cases are assigned to particular judges: Whether the chief judge's office within each competent court assigns cases to judges according to his best judgment (as in Poland), or whether cases are assigned to judges by lottery (as in Ecuador), or electronically (as in Argentina), or whether cases are assigned through other methods. To reduce possibilities of corruption and politicization of decision-making, cases should, to the extent possible, be distributed among judges in a manner that would eliminate "judge-shopping" and the assignment of cases on politically motivated grounds.

Written Versus Oral Procedures. In many developing countries there is still a tendency towards the written pattern of procedure even for acts that in other jurisdictions are of a strictly oral nature, such as witness testimonies. In many instances, questions are submitted in writing and read out to a witness who dictates his/her answers to a court clerk or secretary. This practice may lead to distortions since testimony is often given only in the presence of the secretary of the court in the absence of a judge. Oral evidence is then evaluated by the judge only in the written form. In Indonesia, for example, all pleadings and arguments, except in the first instance, have to be in writing. There is not a slight chance of being heard orally. However, even in cases where the law establishes a mandatory oral procedure, hearings and a trial, judges may not be trained for that purpose. In countries where there are oral arguments, judges have to be trained not to listen passively but to ask questions and participate in what is not a ritual but a working session to clarify issues. Where written pleadings and testimonies are relied on exclusively, judges should be able to examine their possible shortcomings and to request further information when needed.

Evaluation of Evidence. This can pose its own set of challenges. One example is countries like Argentina, Ecuador, or Peru, where judges are rarely present when witnesses give testimony. One result of this practice is the devaluation of the veracity of witness evidence. When judges tend to rely more on written evidence, they receive only what may amount to a fragmented and incomplete version of facts. Often, however, even when judges examine witnesses themselves or are present during the interrogation of a witness by a lawyer, so much time lapses between examining various pieces of evidence that judges frequently lose the thread linking one piece of evidence to another.

Another distortion in the evaluation of evidence appears when judges, as in Egypt, use the process of evaluation of evidence to disguise their inability to deal with unrealistic case loads. Egyptian judges may routinely issue more than a hundred orders a day. Many of these orders simply refer cases on a wide variety of matters—family disputes, tenancy, contracts, or torts—to expert witnesses, appointed by the Ministry of Justice. The explanation seems to be that although judges have a time limit to issue decisions, expert witnesses do not. When a case appears too complicated and the time limit is approaching, judges let experts study the case and then rely heavily on their opinion.

Writing of Decisions, Reasoning and Discretion. One of the critical issues in any legal system is how to bridge the gap between written law and social practices, between abstract principles and economic realities. Nowhere can this be achieved better than in learned judicial decisions. The writing of decisions involves two aspects: (i) the technique of actually writing and organizing a decision, and (ii) the technique of judicial reasoning and the use of discretionary powers. The latter is a particularly acute problem in the formerly socialist countries where, under the previous regime, judges usually did not possess such discretionary powers.

Appeals. The system of appeals tends to be one of the procedural aspects that needs restructuring in many jurisdictions. In most Latin American countries, as well as in Asia and Eastern Europe, appeals are statutory and have very low monetary thresholds. It is far too frequent in Indonesia, Ecuador, Peru, Egypt or Poland that Supreme Courts spend much of their valuable time studying matters of little juridical, economic or social importance. The lack of requisites to grant an appeal or the lack of sanctions for frivolous appeals encourage abuse of this remedy. In inflationary economies it is often considered "good" business practice for a bad faith debtor to delay payment as much as possible. The money that would eventually have to be paid upon final judgment produces enough returns in interest during the delay to compensate the debtor. This practice would be discouraged by a requirement to deposit upon appeal an amount equal to the debt or a portion of it into an escrow account. Another measure could be heavier fines for frivolous appeals that have no other purpose than delaying a final judgment. In Indonesia, for example, the Supreme Court has a backlog of more than 22,000 cases. In Poland, the Administrative Supreme Court has a backlog of around 5,000 cases.

Physical Facilities of Courts

There is widespread belief in many developing countries that the paramount task of judicial reform and modernization of the administration of justice is to construct buildings and equip them with computers and photocopying machines. Sometimes higher salaries, new legislation, and training are added to these goals. While the upgrading of physical facilities alone is rarely the answer to the complex problem of inefficient administration of justice, better facilities and work environment can often contribute to higher motivation and productivity of judges. To give an example, in some courts in Caracas, litigants must wait in line for two hours to enter an elevator in the court building—just to be told, after finally reaching their destination, that the person they want to see is busy or absent that day. This type of ill treatment, which is common in many countries, seriously damages the performance of the courts, the rights of those who use the system, and the general image of the justice system. In many countries, several judges have to share the same office, without privacy to work or to make telephone calls.

The inadequate building facilities in some countries not only affect work conditions for judges, but diminish the dignity of the justice system and at times even affect its security. Many times during hearings, silence is required in a courtroom to evaluate a piece of evidence or listen to an oral argument. Also, a minimum of dignity, comfort, and cleanliness is due to any public function. In Egypt, courts have traditionally closed for most of the summer, as air conditioning is yet to be introduced in courtrooms. In Albania, judges have to work and listen to arguments in hallways of public buildings.

Automation has been of great assistance in simplifying court procedures, organizing work, and reducing the time required to obtain information. Automation can also help to make more transparent the process of assigning and distributing cases to judges. Some successful experiments have been conducted in Argentina to simplify procedures and reduce delays. While automation can be very beneficial to the courts, its utility should not be overestimated, especially in countries where courts lack the elementary facilities and trained personnel required to operate and maintain automated equipment.

Another common problem in practically every developing country is the lack of adequate libraries and archives. Apart from the quality of judges and the propriety of applicable procedures, the quality of a court can virtually be measured by the quality of its library and archives. In the United Kingdom, when Lord Denning turned 80 years old, he was asked why people considered him the greatest English judge since Lord Mansfield. He answered that he had the best law library of all judges. However modest this answer was, it carries a good deal of truth. Judges must at least be able to know the law and how it has been applied and interpreted. This, along with judges' training, is perhaps the most urgent common need in courts around the world.

The Impact of Court Decisions on Society

All previous elements mentioned here are of little use if court decisions do not produce significant effects for the litigants or the society. Many times lawyers, jurists, judges and legal reformers fall into the intellectual temptation of forgetting the real purpose of dispute resolution—to serve the needs of society and provide a remedy to aggrieved parties. Unfortunately, in many countries the judicial process is a complex and costly exercise that leaves litigants in a situation no better than before.

A typical example is the difficulty of enforcing and executing judgments in most of Eastern and Central Europe and many Latin American countries. A common complaint of litigants and business people in Poland, Egypt and Indonesia is that obtaining a favorable judgment from the Supreme Court is only half the way to victory, even if it took several years of court battles. The reasons may vary, but the effect is the same. A banker in Venezuela expressed his feelings that enforcing a judgment was difficult. As a rule he dealt only with people he knew well, even though that meant restricting his business operations. In Peru, for similar reasons, some firms write off debts below a certain amount of money. In Russia, the inability to execute a judgment may lead litigants to circumvent the official justice system and seek the assistance of unofficial or even illegitimate sources. The problems in this area deserve the utmost attention. Without the ability to enforce a judicial judgment properly, the whole exercise can become a purely academic pursuit.

Another example, too common in developing countries, is the low level of monetary compensation for damages—whether tortious or contractual. Judges typically grant damages which do not discourage breaches of contract or negligent behavior. This is the other extreme to the practice in some state courts in the United States where juries often award highly exaggerated damages, often reduced on appeal or in out-of-court settlements.

The above examples demonstrate not only poor education about the economics of the law, but at times the lack of awareness among judges of the enormous discretionary powers that they possess even in civil law systems. Judges have every day the opportunity of becoming relevant to the society in which they live and work.

Alternative Dispute Resolution Mechanisms

If the state does not provide an efficient and socially effective system of administration of justice, the society, unfailingly, would find its way to providing alternative mechanisms for solving disputes. Ideally, this would happen through legally acceptable means like negotiation, conciliation, mediation or arbitration. If such means were not available, however, people may circumvent the official system entirely and resort to illegal means such as intimidation or lynching. Examples are only too familiar. Impatient citizens in the informal urban developments in Lima, Peru, facing an uncontrolled upsurge in crime, several times took justice into their own hands to punish a rapist, thief or murderer. In Jakarta, and other localities of Indonesia, unsatisfied creditors engage gangs of "debt collectors" who bully and threaten overdue or careless debtors. In Russia, some creditors, as indicated above, are reported to have turned to the "mafia" for help.

Alternative dispute resolution mechanisms (ADRs), however, do not have to be a sign of decaying judicial systems that are incapable of meeting the needs of the community. Very often ADRs are useful vehicles assisting judges overloaded with cases. This is also the situation in countries with largely developed judicial systems, where ADRs have proven an indispensable instrument used and encouraged by the courts themselves. Practically everywhere in the world dockets are overcrowded and any form of relief is welcome by those who monitor the performance of courts. Also, judges who understand that their real role in society is not necessarily to write impeccable and long judgments, but to solve disputes according to the law, can encourage parties to submit a dispute to mediation or conciliation or to settle it amicably through negotiations by their counsel when the prospective litigation is going to be costly and time-consuming both for the parties and for the court. Mechanisms for conciliation have always existed in the codes of procedure in most developing countries, but have rarely been used by judges due to the lack of appreciation of their real role or simply due to the lack of training. In the United States, by contrast, in addition to well established private arbitration techniques, the courts have started with court-sponsored ("court-annexed") mediation, conciliation and arbitration programs.

A common feature of countries where the legal system does not adequately meet the needs of society and produces a gap between law and reality (as I am told is the case in most of Latin America) is that the official system of administration of justice is used neither by the very rich and powerful, nor by the very poor, destitute or marginalized members of society. Also, it is not used by groups of people engaged in activities that require specialized knowledge of their work methods and transactions. Indigenous populations, peasant communities, and menbers of the "informal economy," whether in Caracas, Rio de Janeiro, Cairo or Jakarta, have all developed their own spontaneous ways and methods to solve peacefully their differences and disputes. Most of these mechanisms do not have to face the problems of judgment enforcement and execution that ordinary courts face, because they usually receive a high degree of acceptance. In countries where legal and cultural traditions permit it, judges can promote the participation of lay persons in small claims courts and misdemeanor courts. This is, for example, the case of Peru's justices of the peace, who are not only very much immersed in the community, but seem to enjoy more social acceptance than other judges in that country. Over 63 percent of their decisions are not appealed any further.

Another reason certain parties prefer ADRs is that foreign investors may distrust the neutrality of local judges, or domestic business communities may lack confidence in judges' competence in highly technical areas of commercial law. Disputes relating to foreign investment and complex investment, commercial, insurance, banking or securities matters are often referred to commercial arbitration. In the case of disputes between a foreign investor and a host government, arbitration is usually conducted under a foreign or international arbitral system, including the arbitration system of the International Centre for Settlement of Investment Disputes (ICSID), which is connected with the World Bank.

However, even in private arbitration where the whole process takes place outside the state-sponsored judiciary and without court intervention, the state has to intervene if the losing party refuses to abide by the outcome. In those instances the courts have to step in and enforce the award as if it was a court ruling. Disputes are unavoidable in communities, and the fact that most of them never reach a court of law should not be a matter of concern. If disputes can otherwise be settled in a peaceful, equitable, and fair manner, this reduces the need for lengthy judicial proceedings. But in some cases the losing party refuses to comply with the award and courts of law should provide enforcement. This applies also to foreign awards, after the normal review by a local court (except for ICSID awards). Local courts are thus expected to provide assistance, including annulment of the outcome of arbitration when due process has not been observed, and correcting whatever omissions or distortions they may find in the process.

Conclusion

The World Bank's experience in judicial system reform, though limited to a few countries, has included diagnostic studies to better understand the issues involved. Where the administration of justice fails to meet the needs of society, the most common reasons are the following:

- the inadequacy of legislative tools used by judges, compared to the complexities of court procedures;
- the lack of efficient organization of the court system, resulting in overloaded judicial dockets, backlogs and long delays;
- the lack of developed skills among judges to manage workloads efficiently and productively;
- judges' inexperience in exercise of discretionary powers;
- the lack of training in new areas and judges' resistance to hearing cases involving complex legal issues in commercial law;
- the neglect of the judiciary's material and logistic needs;
- the high cost of litigation; and
- in certain countries, corruption that stifles the rule of law.

The lessons outlined here agree for the most part with the findings of comparative studies in other contexts. In Latin America and the Caribbean, as elsewhere, these issues must be addressed by multilateral institutions in order to establish better investment flows to the countries where they are most needed.

CHAPTER 14

Instituto de Cooperación Iberoamericana

Juan Antonio March Pujol

Activities in the justice sector have come to occupy a central place in Spain's policies for development co-operation, for a number of reasons. First of all, we recognize that there is a close relationship between how a society is institutionally structured and its capacity and potential for development. Second, judicial reform affects all other aspects of development, for without secure judicial institutions, one cannot speak of development or of equity.

The present situation regarding development can be compared to a soccer game. A soccer game, as you know, requires a well-demarcated field, two goals, a ball, and referees. Even with these components, you also need 22 players; and the players must know the field boundaries, where to place the ball, and so on. But what seems to be happening now is that the rules of the game are changing due to certain innovations (the type of ball, or the size of the field), and the game itself is becoming more interesting. In effect, the institutional framework is no longer fixed or invariable.

As for how all this affects the justice sector, it is clear that the security of judicial institutions arises from two major sources: the content of the law, and the organization and operation of the legal system. And since both are profoundly affected by changes in the rules of the game, this offers a great opportunity for long-needed reforms in judicial institutions.

To cite a few examples of programs in the justice sector, Spanish cooperation is helping to set up the Constitutional Court in Bolivia and improve registries and cadastres. We are also training judges and introducing oral procedure in Honduras, training justices of the peace in El Salvador, and reforming the criminal code and training criminal law judges in Peru. We have provided technical assistance for new regulations in areas such as privatization and consumer protection, and assisted courts in defending the right to competition in Argentina and Chile. We will soon sign a governability program with the UNDP for 11 million dollars, for projects to strengthen the modernization of justice, social security entities, decentralization, and social equity. We are going to earmark approximately five million dollars in donations for improving justice systems in Central America.

Furthermore, we have a program for harmonizing legislation in the framework of MERCOSUR, and we expect to strengthen joint efforts between the Spanish Agency for International Co-operation and the IDB to establish operational justice programs.

We believe that the focus on specific programs and projects in the area of development assistance will disappear by the end of the century, and that a structural relationship must be forged between donors and beneficiaries. Those countries that want to implement specific policies in a given direction, and are willing to make an effort, will need a commitment from more advanced countries for structural funding to improve their educational sectors, for example, as well as for redesigning the whole institutional framework.

With this in mind, we are creating mixed funds for cooperation between the Latin American countries and Spain that act as structural funds and that are introduced into each country's own development processes. Through these structural funds we will be able to increasingly support the development of the law and the internal organization of the state. We believe that structural funds of this type, which we began to adopt in Spain in 1995 (the first was constructed with El Salvador and the second with Argentina) will continue to be successively implemented in other Latin American countries.

While the approach to development aid has been based primarily on income criteria, we now propose a development assistance policy based on supporting the entrance of these economies into the world economy, and accelerating the processes of development in education, infrastructure, and institutional modernization. We would like to see this development assistance policy become widespread, because it would enable Latin America to regain its place as a major beneficiary of development aid in the next century.

Spanish co-operation has a specific role to play. When the treaty was negotiated whereby Spain joined the European Community, some thought that this meant that Spain would abandon Latin America. We said that the opposite would happen, that relations between Spain and Latin America would actually be strengthened, and the passage of time is showing that was correct. If Spain were not part of Europe now, it would be a perfectly useless country, I would say, for Latin America. The fact of our belonging to the European Union allows us to constantly absorb Nordic, German, British, French, and Italian proposals, which we are integrating and refining; and where we have a comparative advantage is in transmission time. Although a vast amount of information is accessible to the whole world now, certain cultures remain handicapped in respect to transmission time.

Therefore, the information that Spain absorbs in the context of the EU can be rapidly transferred to all of the Latin American countries, and perhaps this is the field that we have adapted to most. In this area, we have developed a whole new system—that up to a certain point can be extrapolated to many Latin American countries—in relation to all of the new regulations that have been analyzed so well here, such as the laws to defend competition, for consumer protection, for managing privatization so as to strengthen equity, and so on.

In 1960, Spain was absolutely broke and had a level of development lower than three countries in Latin America. Our per capita income was less than US$2,000 in 1960. Today, per capita income in Spain is US$14,000. Therefore, we can say that the Spanish development process has been relatively successful. This experience should hold lessons for many countries, especially as regards adapting and reeducating the personnel of state institutions, and modernization of the productive sector.

Finally, regarding the cooperation between the IDB and the bilateral donors, the relationship can be very close. Spain can provide some important aid in the form of technical assistance and training, and the IDB could obviously contribute to this, but above all, could also begin to steer its loans more to strengthening the judiciaries' communication and information systems than to building more costly infrastructure.

Therefore, an interesting and useful dialogue could ensue on this, especially on tax policy, a major issue that must be given priority. Revamping the tax systems is directly related to the administration of justice, and should be put on the agenda. In this way, everything that the bilateral donors do with various countries might also receive significant support from the IDB, especially in providing equipment to those countries that already want to reform or modernize certain institutions.

A related issue is cooperation among the Ibero-American countries. Major strides have been made in this area, as evidenced during the Ibero-American Summit at Bariloche [October 1995]. There a cooperation agreement among 21 Ibero-American countries was signed, opening the doors to coordination of programs to foster social mobility and to promote closer ties among the Ibero-American societies, facilitating the sharing of experience and know-how among them.

These programs include the *Iberoencuentros*, sectoral meetings of groups from the 21 Ibero-American countries, to share experiences and implement Ibero-American cooperation programs. In the areas of justice, harmonization of laws, training of personnel, and human resources management, we believe this approach opens up a new door to radical inquiry within Ibero-America, marked by specific relations among certain countries, and also, especially focused on some northern centers, but insufficiently structured within. It is our impression that relations among Uruguayans, Argentines, Chileans, and Brazilians are very intense, but with Dominicans, Salvadorans, or Peruvians, this is less so. Therefore, if we are moving towards a great era of globalism, we need to have a broader view of cultural identities, which in no way should define themselves as clans, but which allow cultures to see themselves in a broader context. This is the change fostered by the Ibero-American Summit, which has the potential to be extremely useful.

In the words of President Samper at the Bariloche Summit, "Comparative advantages do not exist, they are made." A great challenge faces Latin America in the next century. We are starting from very good foundations, and from the get-go we are banking on democratic systems, institutional modernization, improvements in productive systems, rigorous economic policies, and improved social conditions. However, we must recognize that time is scarce, and that we are about to enter a world of open competition.

It is important to emphasize the impact of institutional reform on productivity. In other words, we must introduce an analysis of the costs entailed in certain procedures, certain consultations, and the security or contributions they confer. The three major topics that must be included in the Ibero-American agenda are integration, modernization, and competitiveness. And since the institutional picture is conditioned by the degree of competitiveness in a given economy, we must find ways to accelerate the transformation of the institutional framework, because it will improve our social conditions and the potential for development of all citizens.

CHAPTER 15

The U.S. Agency for International Development

Paul S. Vaky

Throughout Latin America and the Caribbean, there is growing concern for the rule of law as critical to the development of democracies. An effective judicial system is integral to the economic growth and well-being of a society. As Ambassador James Michel has stated,

> Without strong and respected institutions capable of guaranteeing security of person and property, the aspirations of the people to participate in the benefits of liberty and economic opportunity cannot be realized.... [T]he justice system protects citizens against common delinquency and against arbitrary or corrupt governmental misconduct. It provides an objective forum for resolving disputes on the basis of generally accepted norms, thereby facilitating peaceful commerce, economic competition and productive investment. And it is the justice system to which a citizen can appeal directly, without the intervention of bureaucratic or political or economic patrons, to apply the rule of law to safeguard his own rights.

Moreover, the growing interdependency among nations calls for stable, responsive and competent justice systems. Where such stability does not exist, international commerce and cooperation suffer. And as transnational crime has increased, there is greater demand and need for effective law enforcement.

Reform in the Hemisphere

The region's justice systems have suffered from persistent problems, such as outdated legal codes, lack of trained personnel, poor administration and record keeping, inadequate financial resources, supplies and facilities. The criminal justice sector faces additional obstacles, such as ineffective criminal investigation and prosecution, inadequate public defense efforts, militarized police forces, and antiquated and overcrowded prisons.

In response to these serious difficulties, some progress is taking place. Legal procedures and codes are being revised. The selection and training of judicial officers is improving, and training programs have been implemented to promote more competent civilian police forces. New mechanisms have increased public access to justice, and alternative methods for resolving disputes have been introduced apart from the traditional court system.

Significant code revisions are taking place in Guatemala, Honduras, Costa Rica, Colombia, Bolivia, and Argentina. Virtually every country in the Southern Hemisphere is undergoing serious review of its legal system, including Haiti. Many are considering the implications of moving from an inquisitional system to an adversarial system, which means shifting investigative responsibilities from the judiciary to the prosecutorial staff. Among those are Guatemala, El Salvador, Ecuador, Peru, Bolivia and Argentina. Such a change tends to involve revaluating the role of the police, prosecutors, and judges in the justice system.

Questions have been raised about the efficiency and effectiveness of the courts in Latin America, and whether other methods to resolve disputes should be developed. There is growing awareness of the need to strengthen the integrity of the judiciary. Laws to promote career stability and improved selection processes for judges have been introduced by many countries. The development of a truly independent judiciary is being discussed, which would stabilize the legal system and enhance its credibility.

Increased professionalism and competence of judges, prosecutors, and police is a major concern through the region. Programs to professionalize and increase the capability of a civilian police force are being developed and implemented. The training of judges, prosecutors and police, emphasizing their investigative interaction, is a major concern for many countries.

Some countries are developing active public ministries or attorney general's offices with significant investigative authority, including Colombia, Bolivia, Guatemala and Honduras. Another reform being considered at the same time is an established public defender's office. This would provide legal access to justice for indigents and the poor, and help to counterbalance an activist public ministry.

The rule of law plays an important role in stabilizing a democratic society. But the political will to accept and implement reform efforts is crucial. Linked to political will is commitment and availability of adequate financial and technical assistance.

USAID's Involvement

In the 1960s, USAID's early efforts in justice and development focused on enhancing the capacities of law schools in the developing countries to train lawyers. More recent programs since the mid 1980s have focused on the efficiency of court systems, training for judges, prosecutors and police, developing public defender systems and improving court administration. The overall aim of these programs is to assist the development of effective and equitable systems of justice, in order to protect the rights of the people and to strengthen democracy.

In the last ten years, the Latin American and Caribbean Bureau of USAID has committed over $200 million to justice projects, in which every country in the region (except Cuba and Suriname) has participated to some extent. These projects range from $200,000 for a judicial exchange program in Mexico to a $36 million, six-year project aimed at a multi-dimensional restructuring of Colombia's justice system.

USAID is assisting the government of Colombia to develop its justice system in accordance with sweeping reforms adopted in its 1991 Constitution. These reforms will provide the basis for more efficient and effective administration of justice, founded on an accusatorial system of law. Three new entities were created: the Constitutional Court, the Superior Judicial Council and the "Fiscalia." In collaboration with the Ministry of Justice and the "Procuraria," USAID is helping to train public prosecutors who are taking over the role formerly held by investigative judges. The goal of this training, which includes training the Colombian police, is to increase the effectiveness of the investigation and prosecution of serious crimes. Strengthening the administration, operation and independence of courts is also an integral part of this project.

In Bolivia, USAID has worked with the government since 1992 to develop judicial efficiency and accountability through modernized structure and efficient case processing, effective criminal prosecution and investigation capability of prosecutors and police, through training to improve investigative techniques and case management, preparation and presentation; a public defenders' office on the national level; public education and legal aid; and alternative dispute resolution. To date, over 775 Bolivian lawyers and judges have attended specialized seminars on the advantages of oral process and the legal clinic as an alternative method of training.

In Argentina, USAID funding supported training, research and study in three main areas: court administration, legal aid/mediation and judicial training. In the Caribbean, USAID funded a regional project that included enhancing national libraries, printing and selling legal textbooks and casebooks for regions and countries, developing a computerized system for indexing court judgments, conducting a study of administration records management in Caribbean courts, and training some 880 people in 120 courses for judges, prosecutors, defenders, librarians and paralegals. Jamaica has also begun a mediation program.

As for Haiti, although its situation is unique, it exemplifies the importance of a justice system in the development of democracy. The restoration of democracy in Haiti involves assistance to support private sector development, monitoring elections, job creation and development of public institutions. A key component of USAID's assistance program is to structure a functional judicial system, including a) training of a new civilian police force; b) establishing a judicial training center for all Haitian judges and prosecutors, the technical assistance being provided by the U.S. Department of Justice; c) developing a prison registry system and mechanisms to reduce the number of pre-trial detainees; and d) improvement in the administration of justice, including case management, tracking and reporting. This program has included donor assistance from France and Canada as well.

In Chile, USAID-funded projects had four objectives: 1) conducting training for judicial system personnel while supporting national efforts to establish permanent, publicly funded training for the judicial branch; 2) improving the nationwide judicial library and legal information system; 3) strengthening the administration of the courts; and 4) supporting improvement of legal assistance to the poor through nationwide analysis and pilot efforts to design alternatives for broader access to such assistance.

In Costa Rica, USAID assisted the Judicial School of the Supreme Court to evolve into a professional and efficient education organization, developing a solid program for training judicial officials and administrators. USAID funding also has supported the establishment of an alternative dispute resolution mechanism.

In El Salvador, USAID assistance supports Salvadoran efforts to accelerate and deepen the judicial reform process, including reforms to criminal procedure code, criminal code, criminal sentencing and administrative procedures; training for judges, public defenders, prosecutors and law processors; a public education program; curriculum reform in law schools; development and distribution of legal textbooks; improved court administration; and reducing criminal and civil case backlogs.

In Guatemala, USAID has developed a major project to support implementation of the new Guatemalan criminal procedure code. The Public Ministry has been strengthened and given new criminal investigative authority. The new code also introduces oral process in criminal proceedings. The project provides technical assistance and training for the Public Ministry as well as for the Supreme Court and San Carlos University.

In Honduras, a new criminal code is being drafted. USAID is developing a program of training and technical assistance for the newly formed Attorney General's office and the new civilian investigation unit.

In Panama, USAID assistance has focused on expediting case management and reducing case backlog as well as the development of a civilian police force. This assistance has supported 1) regulations on judicial careers, established and implemented by the Supreme Court; 2) regulations supporting accelerated trial procedures and alternatives to pretrial detention; 3) establishment of new courts,

4) improvement of case processing by both courts and the Public Ministry, and 5) development of a training program for a civilian police force.

In Uruguay, USAID's five-year program centered on improving court administration, training judicial personnel, and taking steps to modify or improve implementation of selected laws affecting commerce.

In addition, USAID has funded a series of conferences throughout the region addressing important aspects of legal reform. Coordinated by the National Center for State Courts, their topics included legal access for the poor, oral proceedings, pre-trial detention, and alternative dispute resolution. Representatives of the entire region attended: nonprofit organizations, private attorneys, law professors, the judiciary, and justice and public ministry officials. These conferences stimulated dialogue and exchange of experiences, as well as identifying issues to be addressed. USAID will prepare a document articulating these findings for distribution.

A particular focus of USAID support has been developing a competent professional police force under civilian control and respectful of human rights, which is essential for the effective and equitable enforcement of the law, a critical element of a capable justice system. Through the Department of Justice International Criminal Investigative Training Assistance Program (ICITAP), USAID has provided funding and technical assistance for the training of civilian police. The purpose is threefold: to enhance professional capabilities in investigative and forensic functions; to assist in developing instruction for law enforcement personnel; and to improve the administrative and managerial capabilities of law enforcement agencies. In this Hemisphere, ICITAP has developed police programs in Bolivia, Brazil, Colombia, Costa Rica, the Dominican Republic, the English-speaking Caribbean, El Salvador, Guatemala, Honduras, Panama, Peru and Venezuela. Fundamental to these programs is the investigation of crime, which is the point of interaction among courts, prosecutors, and police.

In summary, USAID's experience over the past ten years has confirmed that the development of effective judicial institutions is critical to sustain democracy. Change is never easy, and it is especially difficult in an area as sensitive as the law. But legal reforms are vital for democracy in the Hemisphere.

CHAPTER 16

The United Nations
Development Programme

Jorge Obando

Latin American countries have often addressed temporary crises in their justice systems. However, the problems that now pervade the region's judicial sector amount to a structural failure of the institutions themselves. Widespread debate concerning the administration of justice has led to a broad consensus that judicial reform is urgently needed, and that it must be comprehensive. The Regional Office for Latin America and the Caribbean of the United Nations Development Programme has declared its strong commitment to a particular dimension of judicial reform, which is to strengthen the defense of fundamental rights.

We believe that judicial reform has the potential to breathe new life into Latin America's process of institutional development, by providing a legal framework and public forums for transparent and impartial contestation. An effective judicial sector can advance the democratization process in at least three ways, by: (i) responding to social and political demands, in a context marked by efficiency, effective planning, and accountability of government employees (governability); (ii) observing the fundamental rights and guarantees that ensure respect for the human person (the rule of law), and (iii) establishing clear and stable rules to provide security in social interactions and economic transactions (judicial security).

Approach to Judicial Reform

Based on consultations with political leaders and representatives of civil society, the UNDP concluded that programs to transform the justice sector face three basic demands: (i) judicial protection; (ii) legal or judicial certainty; and (iii) commitment. The first of these, the demand for judicial protection, has two dimensions in the scant literature available: protection of citizens from possible abuses of power by different sectors of the state (abuses or deviant exercise of power, administrative corruption, and human rights violations); and the protection of citizens from damage caused by other citizens. This latter dimension, broadly understood, means keeping the social fabric together under current circumstances, which are marked by complex forms of criminal behavior, corporate irresponsibility with respect to the environment, and the tremendous power of organized crime. The demand for judicial protection thus requires institutions capable of reducing social and political conflict to tolerable levels.

Second is the demand for certainty. The transition to democracy, while it begins with free elections and rule of law, entails a profound social reorganization and a transformation in the role of the state. This demand for certainty in the application and observance of written norms can be seen from two perspectives. First, the parties to economic activity, whether global or regional, have a need for transparency, impartiality, and permanance of the rules that affect foreign investment, labor relations, commercial law, and tax law. Latin America's judicial sector has not been effective in establishing clear-cut limits between such economic activity and the intent of constitutional provisions, nor has it assured the timely resolution of conflicts, as proceedings are slow-moving. Second is the perspective of the common citizen who feels that many individual economic rights have become highly uncertain. New labor relations, the regulation of newly privatized services, the preservation of free trade, the need for consumer protection and for limits on taxation, all directly affect the lives of the vast majority of citizens.

The third demand is for commitment. The transition to a democratic society rarely occurs in conditions of social tranquillity; to the contrary, it has seen a string of conflicts and shifts in power relations. Latin America's new constitutions are addressing such conflicts with new institutions, such as the Office of the Ombudsman and the judicial councils (*consejos de la magistratura*). But the lack of harmony and stability calls for a justice system committed to constantly reestablishing the delicate balance in the exercise of executive and legislative powers, and in their relation to the judicial branch.

Addressing these three demands requires coordination and specialization among the international agencies. Two perspectives on development—democratic governability and judicial reform—find common ground in the concept of conflict. The rule of law comes about as the result of a societal effort to achieve social peace, order, security, and progress, by effectively and impartially settling conflicts. On the other hand, the rule of law is undermined when a conflict endures in time without establishing the mechanisms to solve it; and these mechanisms are largely juridical in nature.

Many legal and empirical research studies have concluded that in Latin America the most common approach to understanding violence (between individuals, between individuals and the state, and between states) is not the law, but force or power. In practice this leads to violence, corruption, and impunity, which in turn make the situation even more ungovernable.

The judicial system operates at a second level of response to conflict. Even though less than ten percent of disputes and social conflicts reach the courts, the judiciaries are overwhelmed, in some cases on the verge of collapse. Indeed, in one Central American country, of all the crimes prosecuted from 1984 to 1994, only 21 percent have been the subject of a decision in the courts of first instance. The remaining 79 percent have piled up in the courts without any decision. In the opinion of the dominant thinking, which the UNDP shares, the main obstacles to prompt administration of justice are the inefficiency of investigative mechanisms, and procedures that are slow, cumbersome, and secret.

The third level of conflict resolution, though it should be the first employed for its economy and efficiency, consists of alternative dispute resolution mechanisms (ADR). Such alternative systems are just beginning in countries such as Ecuador and the Dominican Republic, while other countries like Argentina and Colombia have some experience with them. In a legal culture long accustomed to invert the logical order of responding to conflict, rather than take advantage of the most economical and effective means of arriving at solutions, alternative methods of dispute resolution are a welcome development.

To respond effectively to these demands, international assistance in judicial reform should be comprehensive, coordinated, and specialized. Wherever there is a national will to carry out reform, a country should be able to benefit from coordination among the international agencies, and the specialization of each in a given area of reform. Programs to convert or modernize the justice system should not avoid those issues that arouse controversy, such as criminal law procedures or other judicial policies of the state.

Serious academic studies, the reliable communications media, and informed public opinion are all of the view that in Latin America the main factors operating to the detriment of the state are corruption, citizen insecurity, organized crime, and lack of environmental protection. These problems can only be addressed by modern and intelligent criminal and administrative policies. Criminal law and administrative law provide important bases for tackling these problems. The UNDP accords priority to these two dimensions of legal development, which are in accord with the philosophy of our founding charter and the principles on which the United Nations is based. This does not mean that the economic dimension of the law should not benefit from reforms, but rather that the humanization and effectiveness of the criminal and administrative law are of special interest. Democratic governability is only possible if one can live with dignity and security; but of course prosperity is also a primary social interest.

Justification for Support

The UNDP's support for projects aimed at judicial reform has the following purposes and characteristics:

Strategy

- To promote and make effective the concept of the law as a means for social and economic development that guarantees the strengthening of political and economic democracy.
- To strengthen a culture of respect for human rights and swift, impartial, and effective justice.

Tactics

- To strengthen judicial independence, while furthering joint and coordinated action of the justice sector.
- To assist in legal reform.
- To promote the use of alternative dispute resolution mechanisms.
- To support NGOs in particular, and civil society in general, encouraging their participation in modernizing and humanizing the administration of justice and improving access to the system.
- To assist the justice sector in defining strategies that give direction to the processes of development and modernization.

Operations

- To improve administration and management of the organizations in the justice sector.
- To reduce the number of prisoners held without judgment, and to humanize the prison systems.
- To assist in the sustainable development of the human resources of the sector through ongoing training of judicial staff.
- To collaborate with the legislative function in analyzing the proposed legislation submitted by the judiciary or the executive, or originating within the legislature.
- To assist in designing instruments to monitor projects to improve the sector.

Guiding Principles

- Respect for and sensitivity to the particular features of each culture and its legal system.
- Active feedback as to progress made and experiences in both state reform overall and judicial reform, so as to strengthen public trust in the administration of justice.

- Transparency before the beneficiary countries as to the purposes, objectives, and working methods of the projects.
- Ongoing effort to strike a balance between the system's capacity to swiftly and impartially prosecute crime and at the same time, to guarantee the protection of fundamental rights

Operational Principles

- Administration of projects based on medium-term benchmarks.
- Ongoing analysis to design an agenda for change sensitive to each particular situation.
- High level of participation in project implementation by the national authorities of the justice sector, by promoting and forming national coordinating commissions.
- Wise use of computer technology, so as to streamline the process of national indebtedness when the equipment may be suspectible to planned obsolence.
- Comprehensive programs that foster cultural resurgence, legal reform, and improved administration and management, and that give the justice sector an identity of its own.
- Strengthening the design and implementation of coherent and self-sustaining judicial policies.

Specific Advances

The UNDP's specific advances in judicial reform include the process of building up a roster of human resources with strategic, technical, and administrative experience in the field. There are demonstrable results of its efforts to obtain financial resources to implement projects. The technical capacities acquired have been offered to the development agencies and donor countries as tools that may prove useful for project design and implementation. The UNDP will also continue sponsoring international and national forums that facilitate the sharing of experiences with other aid agencies.

CHAPTER 17

The Inter-American Development Bank

Fernando Carrillo

While efforts to control inflation, macroeconomic stabilization, and open trade have clearly shown results in Latin American countries, the same cannot be said of institutional reforms. The reform of government institutions is far more complex, in that it implies restructuring the public sector, or as some say, to vindicate and rehabilitate the state. This is a slow process that requires strengthening the organizations of civil society and encouraging the role of new protagonists in political reforms.

In projects for modernizing the state, the Inter-American Development Bank has followed explicit guidelines, to ensure that the projects converge with economic and social reforms. Judicial reform has a particular set of problems, however, and what succeeds in other areas of public authority does not necessarily apply in the same terms to the judiciary.

Resurrecting the Judiciary

Throughout our region, the judiciary has been the "Cinderella" of the branches of government, the missing player in the process of design, implementation, and evaluation of public policies. For most of this century, the courts have been effectively deprived of jurisdiction over socially relevant conflicts. This helps explain the isolation of the judicial branch and the tendency to conservatism that afflicted our courts for years. The development of the region's legal and judicial systems placed more emphasis on codification and nice-sounding rhetoric than on constitutional rights and guarantees.

In the wake of the Cold War, Latin America's judicial branch resolved to emerge from its sad state of hibernation. A premature appeal to the "end of history" breathed new life into the judiciary's resurrection. But it has ended up looking more like the first day of creation, than a moment for regaining lost opportunities. In other words, many causes of the judicial crisis have persisted, independent of the reform efforts under way. This suggests that, apart from technical and legal considerations, there are specific obstacles to the efficient functioning of judicial institutions.

Defense of Fundamental Rights

The courts have been weak in their ability to protect the fundamental rights of citizens, thereby inhibiting participation in the political arena. The 17 constitutional reforms now under way in the region aim, almost without exception, to strengthen the judiciary and uphold citizens' rights. Economic and social rights have been incorporated in many constitutions, along with mechanisms for participatory democracy. These various types of constitutional provisions are all signs of the resurgence of civil society. They are putting the initiative directly in the hands of new actors, in the context of principles serving the interests of the community, *acciones populares* and class actions.

Broadening Public Access

From a practical standpoint, it is understood that constitutional justice means guaranteeing rights and duties that were hitherto ignored. But ensuring the right of recourse to the courts as a dispute resolution mechanism for the underprivileged is a monumental challenge.

How the courts could empower excluded sectors of the population is not at all clear, nor do we know the best ways of integrating the judiciary into political, economic, and social changes. Major debates have occurred over what some call "judicial activism," an activism that aims to incorporate effective procedural tools into the constitutions, so as to close the gap between the written law and its application in practice

The Role of Judges

In contrast to other areas of state endeavor, judicial reform requires significant involvement of judges and court staff in their actions and decisions, if it is to succeed. Thus proposals for reform must at times reckon with political forces oblivious to the need for autonomous, efficient, and accessible justice.

Judges are called on to demonstrate their independence, opening the courts to those traditionally excluded from its services. At the same time, they are expected to show great efficiency in performing the most traditional service provided by any regime. Statistics for the region show that the greatest burden for judicial systems has been collecting economic debts. The services of the justice system are usually free to those who can obtain them. Thus in many Latin American countries, judicial reform will require budgetary support, to carve out a future space for the reign of justice. In effect, the doctor has been diagnosing the flu, when the people are suffering from a fatal epidemic.

Context and Substance of Reforms

Modernization of legal systems places high priority on updating the laws and ensuring that legal rules take account of many new economic realities and their implications for judicial decisions. Equally important is the administrative strengthening of the judiciary, so as to bolster its capacity for self-government, independence, and autonomy. The fact that these processes are recent makes them no less important. (In fact, most European countries did not begin to strengthen their judicial systems until the postwar period.)

In the case of Latin America, judicial reform was not undertaken until the last decade. The introduction of new instruments involving the participation of civil society, such as alternative dispute resolution mechanisms—mediation, conciliation, arbitration, and friendly settlement—indicate that the social relevance of the judiciary is finally emerging.

Similarly, work with the human factor, civics education, the education and training of human resources, dialogue with bar associations, judges' schools, judges as a professional group, and access to justice now seem to be banal propositions on which we all have very clear positions. Having identified problems and solutions makes it clear that the road ahead is no longer one of assessments. Decisions must be made regarding the mechanisms and means to assure successful reforms.

Direction of Reforms

Reform programs for the justice system are not limited to those that use economic efficiency as the key criterion for evaluating a given judicial reform. Clearly, economic efficiency must be combined with the principles of effectiveness, equity, transparency, citizen participation, and subsidiary role that now define what is meant by good governance and improving the quality of public policies.

Many issues now on the regional agenda will ultimately depend on revitalizing the justice system. These include free trade, which can only proceed smoothly in a context of modern legal systems capable of setting the rules and solving the many disputes that will begin to occur; defining the investment climate in our countries, which requires legal and judicial procedures that are transparent, certain, and predictable when it comes to protecting foreign investment; redesigning a government that pursues fair competition, equity, and environmental protection; and, finally, fighting organized crime, including corruption, which has stepped up its actions. Given this state of affairs, who can't convince a minister of finance of the importance of investing in the justice sector?

Very soon, private international law in Latin America will be in need of uniform rules and procedures that allow judges and lawyers from different lands to speak the same legal language. Similarly, the struggle against the worst forms of crime will involve the creation of international jurisdictions capable of combating the impunity of drug-traffickers in the South and money-launderers and arms traffickers in the North. It should be possible to lower legal borders so as to design a regulatory state capable of redefining its role in the private sector, and with a view to social objectives that were previously blurred by interventionism.

Challenges of Reform

Such future developments will provide new challenges for a second stage of judicial reforms. The second wave of reforms should be characterized by criteria of selectivity, gradual change, and ongoing evaluation of successes and failures. These are complex operations that will yield results in the long term, and some initiatives will require work in specific areas of the legal system. Closer coordination will be required of the various bilateral and multilateral financing agencies to avoid duplication, contradictions, and squandering of resources.

Likewise, an ongoing effort is needed to gauge national commitments, in the executive, legislative, and judicial branches, and the countries' commitments in terms of civil society. Strengthening the organizations of civil society is the other side of the processes of state modernization, and civil society plays an essential role in consolidating judicial reforms. Only with broad national consensus and the backing of political and business leaders, political parties, and mass media is it possible to tackle the complex tasks of judicial reform.

In addition, the international organizations need to respond to countries' requests and be held accountable to them. Seeking and forging a political consensus to legitimate programs for reform is the best way to ensure their success.

The IDB's Activities in the Region

The Bank has held workshops to create national and local consensus in countries such as Colombia, Honduras, and Costa Rica, which has helped to define the components of reform projects implemented in those countries. Based on the requirements of each country involved, there are IDB projects under way that meet the specific needs of its judiciary. At this time the Bank is working in 14 Latin American countries to set in motion the operational tools available to the Bank. Some of these programs introduce specific mechanisms for strengthening alternative dispute resolution, such as the operations of the Multilateral Investment Fund (MIF), particularly in Costa Rica, Colombia, and Peru.

In Costa Rica, a program for the modernization of the judicial administration is also in place that was approved by the Bank's Board of Executive Directors. In El Salvador, progress has been made on one of the components that is at the core of the efforts required to modernize the institutions and the legal reasoning undergirding judicial decisions, such as the substantive and procedural legal reforms needed as a starting point for reforming the management and administration of justice. In Honduras, a project is in place to modernize laws and codes, including instruments to ensure access to justice, accompanied by a strategy, to which resources have been earmarked, to build the organizational infrastructure needed for sound judicial management. In Colombia, one component of the justice project is aimed at increasing the capacity for management and organization of the Office of the Public Prosecutor (Fiscalía General de la Nación), an institution that was created by the 1991 Colombian Constitution to fight crime; the component includes training, the creation of statistical information systems, and participation in policies to assure citizen security.

The Bank also finances broader programs, such as the program for state modernization in Paraguay. This project includes a significant contribution from the Institute for Ibero-American Cooperation for modernizing the registry system. It will advance judicial management by establishing computerized statistical systems, providing for "judges of the peace," and preparing plans for additional infrastructure.

Judicial reform projects are under negotiation or being prepared in the countries of Nicaragua, Panama, and Ecuador. In Argentina, a project is planned with the provincial justice system. A program in Chile is on hold while constitutional and statutory reforms proceed. In Uruguay, the sectoral program includes resources for reform of the judicial system. The Bank's projects in Peru emphasize the management of judicial offices. Finally, the Bank is supporting an arbitration program in Mexico, to help strengthen mechanisms created for that purpose.

Conclusion

Insofar as judicial institutions become stronger and more independent, they should be able to serve public needs more effectively. Douglass North, a leading expert in the economic analysis of institutions, has explained this in terms of both formal and informal rules. What some have called "judicial activism," far from breaching the constitutional provisions so dear to Latin American legal systems, in recent years has set a standard in the exercise of judicial actions—motions to protect rights known variously as *tutelas de derechos, amparos constitucionales*, and *recursos de protección*—unprecedented in Latin America's judicial history.

Moreover, the newly created judicial organs in Latin America have a growing role in the struggle against corruption and organized crime. Where this trend is heading is not yet clear. Although economic efficiency need not be the guiding criterion or the *sine qua non* for judicial reforms, the difficulty of quantifying their results must in no way frustrate the reforms. We should hold to the notion that there can be results, and that they can be quantified, if not correlated economically.

This last point is the major challenge faced by an economic analysis of the law, as well as the temptation to establish an equivalence, for example, between the justice service and traditional public services. The economic evaluation specific to other public services cannot be applied to the judiciary, which is a "public good" or, as economists say, a "merit good." Where justice is involved, equity criteria must serve as a counterweight to the principles of economic efficiency. This is not to deny the need to base strategy primarily on an analysis of political economy and, when possible, on management and results indicators as well.

The "new judge" we imagine must display independence and autonomy in the exercise of his function. Such a person will need interdisciplinary training, as well as personal and economic security. He or she will be a conciliator who can set in motion any of the judicial or extrajudicial dispute settlement mechanisms, and can adequately analyze international issues. Finally, the judge of tomorrow, in addition to displaying probity and transparency, must take responsibility for the social and economic implications of case decisions. Otherwise, one will fall into reformist rhetoric, which Octavio Paz once described as "the trap of constitutionally installed lies."

Contributors

Alberto Alesina
Professor of Economics, Harvard University
Cambridge, Massachusetts

Edgardo Buscaglia
Professor, Georgetown University

Fernando Carrillo
Senior Advisor, State and Civil Society Division
Inter-American Development Bank
Former Minister of Justice, Colombia

Jorge Correa Sutil
Professor
Universidad Diego Portales
Santiago, Chile

Hernando De Soto
Director, Instituto Libertad y Democracia
Lima, Peru

Ricardo Hausmann
Chief Economist
Inter-American Development Bank

Rudolf Hommes
Rector, Universidad de los Andes
Bogotá, Colombia

Tomás Liendo
Secretary for Legal, Technical, and Administrative Coordination,
Ministry of the Economy, Argentina

Néstor Humberto Martínez
Attorney
Former Minister of Law and Justice, Colombia

Jorge Obando
Advisor to the Regional Office for Latin America and the Caribbean,
United Nations Development Programme

Luis Pásara
Consultant, Inter-American Institute of Human Rights
and Andean Commission of Jurists, Peru

Santos Pastor
Director, Economics Department
Universidad Carlos III
Madrid, Spain

Juan Antonio March Pujol
Director General
Instituto de Cooperación Iberoamericana
Madrid, Spain

Miguel Rodríguez
Chief, Trade Unit
Organization of American States

Robert Sherwood
International Business Counselor

Ibrahim Shihata
Senior Vice President and General Counsel
The World Bank

Paul S. Vaky
Attorney, Criminal Division, U.S. Department of Justice
Former Advisor to Latin America and the Caribbean Bureau,
U.S. Agency for International Development